Guild-Ridden Labor Markets

Guild-Ridden Labor Markets
The Curious Case of Occupational Licensing

Morris M. Kleiner

2015

W.E. Upjohn Institute for Employment Research
Kalamazoo, Michigan

Library of Congress Cataloging-in-Publication Data

Names: Kleiner, Morris M., author.
Title: Guild-ridden labor markets : the curious case of occupational licensing / Morris M. Kleiner.
Description: Kalamazoo, Michigan : W.E. Upjohn Institute for Employment Research, [2015] | Series: WE focus series | Includes bibliographical references and index.
Identifiers: LCCN 2015039026 | ISBN 9780880995016 (pbk. : alk. paper) | ISBN 0880995017 (pbk. : alk. paper)
Subjects: LCSH: Occupations—Licenses—History | Professions—Licenses—History. | Guilds—History.
Classification: LCC HD3629 .K54 2015 | DDC 331.702—dc23
LC record available at http://lccn.loc.gov/2015039026

© 2015
W.E. Upjohn Institute for Employment Research
300 S. Westnedge Avenue
Kalamazoo, Michigan 49007-4686

The facts presented in this study and the observations and viewpoints expressed are the sole responsibility of the author. They do not necessarily represent positions of the W.E. Upjohn Institute for Employment Research.

Cover design by Alcorn Publication Design.
Index prepared by Diane Worden.
Printed in the United States of America.
Printed on recycled paper.

Contents

Acknowledgments vii

1 **Anatomy of Occupational Licensing** 1
　Incentives for Regulation 4

2 **The Evolution of Occupational Licensing** 9
　Case Studies of Occupations Seeking Licensure 15
　Summary and Conclusions 22

3 **The Costs, Mobility, and Quality of Occupational** 25
　Licensing Services
　Influence on Wages and Employment 30
　Influence on Geographic Mobility 31
　Influence on Prices 35
　Occupational Licensing as Social Insurance 36
　Influence on Quality of Services 38
　The Net Effects of Occupational Licensing 43
　Conclusions 43

4 **Battles among Licensed Occupations** 47
　Health Care 47
　Licensed and Certified Occupations in Construction— 50
　　Architects versus Interior Designers
　Licensed Occupations That Do Similar Tasks—Physical 53
　　Therapists and Occupational Therapists
　Institutional Background 55
　Conclusions 58

5 **Occupational Licensing in Different Institutional and** 61
　International Contexts
　Occupational Regulation in the European Union 62
　Another Example: Occupational Licensing in the United Kingdom 68
　Institutional Details of Occupational Regulation in the 70
　　United Kingdom
　Nontraditional Licensing: China 72
　Summary and Conclusions 76

6	**Policy Implications of the Evolution of Occupational Licensing in the United States and Elsewhere**	79
	The Federal Role	83
	At the State Level	86
	International Policy Issues	88
	Summary and Implications for U.S. Occupational Licensing Policy	89

References	95
Author	105
Index	107
About the Institute	117

Figures

3.1	Share of Workforce Licensed, by State (%)	29
3.2	Occupational Licensing and Interstate Migration, 1950–2008	32

Tables

3.1	Percentage of Workers Who Require Specific Education and Testing to Become Licensed or Certified	28
5.1	Licensed Occupations in the EU-27, 2012	64
5.2	Prevalence of Occupational Regulation in EU-27 Countries, 2012	66

Acknowledgments

The purpose of the book is to summarize the research and policy issues on occupational licensing in the United States and other countries. The book is nontechnical and is intended for practitioners and those interested in the roles of public policy and labor market institutions on labor markets and society.

I want to thank the staff at the Upjohn Institute for their assistance, especially Randy Eberts, Kevin Hollenbeck, Brad Hershbein, and Linda Richer. I also greatly appreciate the outstanding efforts by Allison Hewitt Colosky; her excellent editing and comments improved the content. Richard Wyrwa offered insightful ideas and support during the writing process. The intellectual environment provided by the economists and staff at the Upjohn Institute greatly enhanced my productivity.

I am most fortunate to have had outstanding collaborators and coauthors while developing the research approaches that are cited in the book. My colleagues at the Federal Reserve Bank of Minneapolis, the Humphrey School of Public Affairs and the Center for Human Resources and Labor Studies at the University of Minnesota, and the National Bureau of Economic Research provided many helpful comments.

Jim and Sheryl Siegel and their family were terrific hosts during my travels to the Upjohn Institute in west Michigan. I thank Sally Mosow Kleiner for her encouragement, technical knowledge, and editorial support. The book is dedicated to my children, their spouses, and my grandchildren, who were most supportive as I worked on various versions of the book.

Chapter 1
Anatomy of Occupational Licensing

Dentists, doctors, lawyers, hair braiders, tour guides, upholsterers, and horse tooth filers are now licensed occupations in either all or some U.S. states. In states where occupations are licensed, the rationale for meeting the requirements is sometimes inconsistent. For example, in Minnesota, it usually takes more direct classroom time hours to become a cosmetologist than a lawyer. In other states, it takes twice as many hours of training to become a manicurist than a paramedic (Dranias 2007). In Louisiana, the only state in the country that requires licenses for florists, monks were until recently forbidden to sell coffins because they were not licensed funeral directors (Carpenter et al. 2012). Nationally, in the 1990s, one could become a physical therapist with just a bachelor's degree, but by 2016, in order to become a fully licensed physical therapist in most states, a practitioner must have a doctor of physical therapy degree, which requires a four-year college degree plus three years of graduate training and work.

These regulations are not just unusual cases of state laws run amok. Instead they reflect policies deriving from one of the fastest growing labor market institutions in the United States—the government licensing of jobs and work tasks. This form of regulation, largely established by state governments and implemented through their licensing boards, is often referred to as "the right to practice." Under these laws, working for pay in a licensed occupation is illegal without first meeting government standards. Certification, another form of government regulation, provides a "right to title" and does not forbid others from providing the service.

In the 1970s, about 10 percent of individuals who worked for pay required licenses, but by 2008, that number rose to almost 30 percent (Kleiner and Krueger 2013). By the turn of the century, more than 800 occupations, including shampoo specialists and professional wrestlers, in addition to the occupations mentioned above, were licensed in at least one state (Carpenter et al. 2012). More workers are directly impacted by occupational licensing than the minimum wage or unionization (Kleiner and Krueger 2010).

Occupational licensing has had a curious and unusual history in the United States and in other countries. During some periods it all but disappeared, but now in the United States it is a rapidly growing labor market institution. For some occupations, such as physicians, it has dominated the labor market and its effects on consumers. For others, such as interior designers, occupational licensing has been limited to a small number of U.S. states. This book addresses several questions regarding how and why some occupations became heavily regulated while others did not. Why do some countries have lots of occupations that are licensed and others a relatively small number? Why has occupational licensing grown over the past 50 years and unions have declined? What are its economic effects on mobility, wage determination, prices, and the quality of services delivered? Occupational licensing, in spite of its growth, size, and economic impact, has been a stealth form of regulation. In this book, I examine why the institution of occupational licensing has had such a curious evolution and influence in the United States, the European Union, and China, and I discuss the many similarities it has to guilds.

With growth of licensing laws has come a national patchwork of stealth regulation that has, among other things, restricted labor markets, innovation, and worker mobility. There is little reason, for example—political, economic, or safety related—for math teachers to be relicensed every time they move from one state to another. These requirements put additional burdens on teachers who are moving across state lines, such as more course work, state residency requirements, and often additional exams, all of which reduce the ability of good teachers to find work faster and students to have high-quality instructors.

Having more flexible reciprocity between states for occupations such as teachers, physicians, or dentists would allow these professionals to move to jobs more efficiently. But perhaps even better would be for states to certify jobs that are currently licensed—such as tour guides, hair braiders, travel agents, or locksmiths—jobs that pose minimal risk of harm to the public and that could better serve customers with a lesser form of regulation.

The political economy of occupational licensing has evolved so that both liberals and conservatives have come to oppose certain elements of it. Many on the left are concerned about individuals raising prices for the essential services of licensed plumbers or electricians and the availability of essential services for those in or near poverty. Many licensed professions are relatively low-skilled jobs, such as barbers, manicurists, nurse's aides, and cosmetologists. The social costs of a bad haircut may be negligible, but the social costs of creating additional employment barriers for disadvantaged populations are not. Many education requirements, continuing education courses, and residency requirements restrict entry into occupations that are the most accessible for low-income individuals. Licensure laws often exclude ex-felons—defensible in many professions but not in all—and such prohibitions make it extremely difficult for ex-offenders to find postprison employment, thereby contributing to America's high recidivism rate (Raphael 2014). On the right, public interest groups such as the Institute for Justice have opposed occupational licensing based on economic liberty arguments, arguing that it reduces economic efficiency and retards economic growth (Carpenter et al. 2012).

There is good reason for workers in licensed fields to push for licensing laws. More occupations in a service-oriented economy are likely to be licensed than in manufacturing. With the shift to more service jobs from 40 percent in 1950 to more than 60 percent in 2007, occupational licensing has grown (Edlin and Haw 2014). As I found when I examined these issues with Princeton economist Alan Krueger, former treasury official and head of President Obama's Council of Economic Advisers, occupational licensing raises wages by 10 to 18 percent (even controlling for factors such as age, education, and other market variables) and raises benefits for licensed workers (Gittleman,

Klee, and Kleiner 2015; Kleiner and Krueger 2013). This is largely due to the ability of regulated professions working through state legislators and regulatory boards to limit the supply of practitioners and eventually drive up costs to consumers.[1]

For more necessary services, such as dentistry, less competition brought about by licensure may drive prices beyond the means of individuals with low incomes. Consumers who cannot afford licensed professionals may do the work themselves. For example, David Kruithoff, a farmhand in Michigan, gave himself a root canal because he said he could not afford a licensed dentist (Kleiner 2006).

INCENTIVES FOR REGULATION

From the time of medieval guilds, service providers have had strong incentives to create barriers to entry for their professions in order to raise wages (Ogilvie 2014). These guilds offered an effective mechanism where guild members and politicians could collaborate in capturing a larger slice of the economic rents and redistributing it to themselves at the expense of the rest of the economy. As Ogilvie (2014) notes, guilds are not just historical curiosities, they have wider implications for the role of institutions in economic growth.

Dartmouth economist Charles Wheelan's research on licensed and unlicensed professions in Illinois finds that the stronger a profession's political organization, the more likely it is to become licensed (Wheelan 1998). He showed that respiratory therapists who organized themselves, and raised their profession's dues in order to lobby for licensing laws, tended to be more successful in getting these statutes passed.

In contrast, consumers who will be affected by the slightly higher costs of, for example, haircuts, are unorganized and arguably underrepresented in the political process. The willingness of a legislature to pass licensure laws without a rigorous analysis of its benefits relative to costs, or the alternatives of less rigorous forms of regulation, creates the opportunity for well-organized producer groups to lobby for laws that will likely bring them personal gain. The arguments for occupational licensing policies are that purveyors of a service have greater information about the quality of the service and can take advantage of consumers over both price and quality. Also, all consumers do not demand the same level of quality. When members of the legal profession told the Nobel laureate Milton Friedman that every lawyer should be of Cadillac quality (a high-priced luxury brand car), he famously replied that many people would be better off with a Chevy (a cheaper but clearly functional alternative). If licensure "improves quality" simply by restricting entry into the profession, then some consumers will be forced to pay for more "quality" than they want or need (Friedman 1962).

There have been, however, movements toward stopping or reducing the growth of occupational regulation in the United States. For example, during the 2012–2013 legislative sessions, Iowa Governor Terry Branstad vetoed the licensing of addictive disorder counselors and other related occupations (Branstad 2013). In Indiana, Governor Mike Pence initially vetoed the licensing of diabetes counselors, anesthesiologist assistants, and dietitians but a year later signed similar legislation. In their messages to the legislature (in each case, legislatures were dominated by their own parties), both Branstad and Pence mentioned that this type of regulation would result in economic losses to consumers, higher prices, and less employment (Associated Press 2013). More recently, in Idaho, Governor Butch Otter vetoed the licensing of sign-language interpreters during the 2015 legislative session (Reynolds 2015). In the eyes of these three governors, the promised benefit of potentially better quality and health and safety was, in their view, far smaller than the costs inflicted on the citizens by unneeded regulation.

Unlike the United States, China (along with most other countries), has national licensing for its regulated occupations. An unusual case study is Poland, which is in the process of deregulating many of its national occupational labor markets (Kleiner and Lachowska

2014). In October 2011, Poland's national government presented an ambitious agenda of deregulating entry to many occupations. By late 2015, the government plans to liberalize the access to about 250 out of the 380 currently regulated occupations. The prime minister's office has stated that liberalizing access to occupations is expected to lead to higher employment, higher-quality services, lower prices, and lower governmental administrative costs. The first phase loosened access to 51 professions; it was passed by the Polish Parliament in April 2013 and signed into law in July 2013. The liberalization of access to 33 of these first 51 liberalized occupations went into effect in August 2013. For the remainder, the new legislation went into effect in January 2014. The range of partially or totally deregulated professions is diverse as well as varying in the degree of deregulation. Among professions strongly affected by the liberalization are attorneys, solicitors, notaries, court clerks, realtors, taxi drivers, excursion guides, employment agents, and body guards. The implementation and evaluation of these occupations should be an interesting and informative case study of the influence of the deregulation of occupations.

Some state governors, the Federal Trade Commission, and the Institute for Justice, a public interest nonprofit legal organization that handles legal cases for individuals involved in occupational licensing disputes among other libertarian issues, are naturally wary of producer groups. Organizations such as the American Society of Interior Designers are seeking licensure for interior designers in all states. They are attempting to present evidence on how potentially harmful certain professions are to the public, while simultaneously arguing that all existing practitioners of these potentially dangerous professions be exempted from the proposed licensure requirements.

Given its importance to the economy and labor market, occupational licensing is an institution that has largely been ignored as a factor that may influence employment, wages, prices, innovation, access, and quality. The purpose of this book is to give the public, consumers, and students of the labor market a detailed nontechnical look at and an examination of the curious institution of occupational licensing in the United States, China, and the European Union. Occupational licensing is rarely discussed and does not receive the media attention that its size and scope warrant. The book will provide an examination of the institution of occupational licensing from a historical perspective, a rationale for the existence of occupational licensing, an international perspective, a view from the perspective of consumers, and finally, some unintended consequences of policies that have occurred to deal with issues that have arisen because of occupational licensing. Readers of this book, be they members of a regulated occupation, consumers, or voters who influence policy, will become more informed about the curious guildlike institution of occupational regulation in the United States and elsewhere.

Note

1. An alternative explanation of this wage growth could be that training and education enhance the value of services provided by regulated practitioners, and as a consequence these individuals may earn more than their unlicensed counterparts.

Chapter 2
The Evolution of Occupational Licensing

Those who cannot remember the past are condemned to repeat it.
–George Santayana (1905, p. 284)

If we look at recent characteristics of occupational licensing, we see various stages of its evolution and history. In the fictional short story and subsequent film "The Curious Case of Benjamin Button" (Fitzgerald 2008), the main character is living his life in reverse—he begins his life as an old man and then grows younger. He finds the right age for his true love (who is living life in the traditional manner, going from young to old) not at the beginning or end of his life, but in the middle. In the case of licensing, it is a labor market institution that has been growing over time while unions have been in a state of decline (Ham and Kleiner 2007; Kleiner and Krueger 2013). Unions and licensing were intersecting during the 1970s through the 1990s, and when these two institutions interact, their influence in the labor market raises wages for those fortunate enough to be in both a unionized and licensed job (Kleiner and Krueger 2010; Gittleman and Kleiner, forthcoming).

Understanding the development of occupational regulation is an important element in understanding its effects in the labor and product markets, as well as how public policies have evolved and how they may be changed. This is especially the case for states, such as Colorado, that have been able to establish rigorous methods to evaluate the efficacy of occupations seeking to become licensed. In this chapter I present a historical background for the evolution of occupational regulation and then give specific examples of occupations (physicians, mortgage brokers, and interior designers) that have moved from no or little regulation to full-blown levels of occupational licensing for all in the occupation.

Milton and Rose Friedman, in their book *Free to Choose* and later 10-part television documentary series that was first broadcast in 1980, shared their views of political economy. One chapter (or segment, in the documentary series) dealt with occupational licensing and the relationship with unions. The segment in the commentary by Friedman begins as follows:

> Hippocrates and his followers started medicine on the road forward to becoming a science. When Hippocrates died at the age of 104, or so legend has it, this "Greek" island was full of medical people, his students and disciples. Competition for customers was fierce. Some 20 years after he died they got together and constructed a code of conduct. They named it the Hippocratic Oath, after their old teacher and master. Every new physician, before he could start practice, came to this spot here in front of those columns and took the Oath. The oath was full of fine ideals for protecting the patient. But it also had a couple of other things in it.
>
> Listen to this one, "I will impart a knowledge of the art to my own self and those of my teachers and to disciples bound by a stipulation and oath according to the law of medicine, but to none others." Today we'd call that a closed shop. Or listen to this one referring to patients suffering from the agonizing disease of kidney or bladder stones: "I will not cut persons laboring under the stone but will leave this to be done by men who are practitioners of this work." A nice market-sharing agreement between physicians and surgeons. Hippocrates must turn in his grave when a new class of medical men takes that oath. After all, he taught anyone, provided only they pay his tuition. He would strongly have objected to the kind of restrictive practices that physicians all over the world have adopted to protect their custom.
>
> In the United States the American Medical Association has for decades been one of the strongest labor unions in the country, keeping down the number of physicians, keeping up the costs of medical care, preventing competition by people from outside the profession with those in it; all, of course, in the name of helping the patient.
>
> Without warning, anyone of us may suddenly need medical care. If we do, we want the very best care we can get. But who can give us that care?

Is it always a graduate of an expensive medical school who has a union card called a medical license? Or might it be someone like this, a trained paramedic working for a private-enterprise organization rendering emergency care? The sweeping statement I make is that the prosperity of this country derives primarily from freedom of enterprise and freedom to hire, to employ, to work, and not from restrictive measures imposed by trade unions. (Friedman and Friedman 1980)[1]

The link between licensing and unions is obvious. Traditional economic theory has generally treated the actions of trade unions in the labor market as a variant of monopoly behavior in product markets (Cartter 1959). For example, at the time of contract negotiations, the trade union acts as a single voice representing its members, and consequently, the employer is faced with a single seller of labor. Furthermore, both institutions have legal protections. This has similarities with licensing, but with licensing there are few sellers at a given wage. This is likely to occur because fewer workers are willing to work because of the government-granted monopoly that limits new entrants and makes being in the occupation more expensive in part because of continuing education and annual state-mandated fees. Subsequent analysis by Freeman and Medoff (1984) argues that unions have both a monopoly and voice effect. The monopoly effect is similar to that presented by Cartter, who suggests that supply is reduced but the voice effect provides benefits beyond just the financial ones. These benefits include grievance procedures and the ability to have seniority determine promotions and wages rather than having them assigned only by the employer.

Unions also can engage in concerted activities, such as strikes or work to rule, that can raise the cost to the firm of employing organized workers relative to nonunion ones. If the companies or plants want to avoid these concerted activities, they have to pay the higher wage and benefit package. Therefore, unions have the ability to reallocate a firm's resources away from shareholders, profits, or capital investment and toward workers. Recent estimates of these reallocations are the present value equivalent of $40,500 per worker in 1998 dollars over the duration of the worker's employment with the firm (Lee and Mas 2012). To the extent that economic rents are present in the firm because of patents, location advantages, or economies of scale, unions are able to reallocate part of those resources to union members. In addition, unions in the private sector are given legitimacy and certain levels of economic protection through federal legislation, such as the National Labor Relations Act (Kleiner and Weil 2012).[2] In the public sector, laws governing unions are established at the state level. Consequently, through their ability to monopolize labor at the firm level and public policy protections through federal and state statutes, unions also should be able to drive up wages and benefits.

Recent histories of the evolution of guilds in the Middle Ages suggest that they evolved in large part to protect from competition the makers of small crafts and businesses, such as blacksmiths and furniture makers (Friedman 1962; Humphris 2013). The guilds argued that they were mainly protecting the public from incompetent or unscrupulous purveyors of products or services. In order for quality to be high, only the skilled craftsman of the particular guild could provide the service. As long as there were small enterprises and persuasive enforcement mechanism by the guild, along with the political power of the local political establishment, these enterprises were able to maintain the largely monopoly power of the guild system throughout Europe.

With the advent of the Industrial Revolution in both the United Kingdom and the United States, smaller enterprises that competed at the local level gave way to larger enterprises, such as car manufactures or steel mills, whose markets were national or international. Consequently, the ability to control markets was much more difficult. Workers in these industrial enterprises did many of the same tasks established by the enterprise and no longer needed guilds. It became much harder to restrict entry or impose governmental entry requirements on these large enterprises, and therefore, in a largely industrial economy, occupational guilds declined (Ogilvie 2014).

During the 1830s and through the later part of the nineteenth century, there were few occupations in the United States that were licensed. In response to Jacksonian populism, the dominant view about government within the political economy and politics at the time was that few occupations should be licensed by the states. Nevertheless, in the late 1800s, several states established educational criteria for the licensing of physicians. In 1882, a physician by the name of Frank Dent wanted to practice medicine in West Virginia, but he had credentials from another state, and the medical school that he had attended was not recognized in West Virginia. Dent was convicted, and his medical license was revoked.

The case reached the Supreme Court, and the Court unanimously upheld the law in West Virginia, establishing the right of states, rather than the federal government, to grant licenses; thus, in 1889, *Dent v. West Virginia* 129 U.S. 114 (1899) was issued. The decision established that state law purporting to protect the health, welfare, or safety of citizens was justified as having a rational relationship to the legitimate end of government under the police powers of the states (Gross 1984). This took away the federal right of preemption in the arena of occupational licensing and gave it to the states. This is different from most other later labor laws, such as the National Labor Relations Act, which established federal law over any state provisions dealing with the regulation of unions and management on collective bargaining. The implication was that each state could establish the level of entry barriers, maintenance for remaining licensed, and the penalties for practicing without having a license.

In response to the changes that occurred during the Progressive Era, as epitomized by President Theodore Roosevelt, more states began to regulate and license more occupations. The Sherman Antitrust Act was passed in 1890, and there was a significant change in the number of occupations that became licensed. In his article "Freedom of Contract," law professor Lawrence Friedman (1965) relates the major legal principles on licensing and other labor reforms that were taking place during this period.

> In the same period, 1890 to 1910, occupational licensing first achieved a firm foothold in the statute-books of most American states. Laws to license doctors, plumbers, barbers, funeral directors, nurses, electricians, horseshoers, dentists, and the practitioners of many other occupations were debated, propounded and very often passed. Many of these laws gave rise to constitutional test cases. Unlike the more spectacular labor law cases, the licensing cases called down no pronouncements of doom and enlisted neither proponents nor opponents in high and academic places to argue validity and propriety on the basis of first principles. This was a quieter, blander area of constitutional law. From the standpoint of logic and of life, however, the cases involved first principles no less than those which arose under wage and hour laws. If a workman had a constitutional and God-given right to work eleven hours a day in a bakeshop, or to be paid in kind instead of cash, he should have had a similar right to contract with an unlicensed barber or to buy a laxative from a druggist without a certificate on his wall. (p. 489)

During this period, physicians and dentists in the United States achieved nearly universal licensing. However, occupational licensing was mainly confined to a few occupations in health and law. Following World War II and the move to a service-oriented economy, there was a resurgence of occupational licensing in which the government—largely at the state level—determined the entry requirements and the criteria to remain a member in good standing within an occupation. The service sector then was much like the medieval guilds—they operated in local markets and could control entry by working with local politicians and representatives of the occupations to promote occupational licensing laws. A standard method of getting an occupation license involved forming an association and establishing a dues collection mechanism, part of which could be used to lobby both legislative and executive branches of state government. Because fees from licensed members of the occupation are greater than the cost of monitoring the licensing provisions of the occupation, the government entity doing the licensing is more likely to gain revenue as a consequence of this form of regulation. The process provides an incentive for members of the occupation, government officials, and the executive branch of government to pass and sign licensing legislation. Even when a governor such as Mike Pence of Indiana is convinced of the negative consequences of the law, political factors often tend to dominate the process. In his case, he initially vetoed and then signed legislation that licensed several health-related occupations.

CASE STUDIES OF OCCUPATIONS SEEKING LICENSURE

Since all occupations reach varying levels of regulation in different ways, I will present background for three occupations—physicians, mortgage brokers, and interior designers—and show how they evolved into full licensure. Specifically, I provide information on the evolution of licensure of these occupations across a continuum of regulation, and I show how regulation influences a variety of occupations at various stages of regulation.

Physicians

By definition, a person licensed to practice medicine is a medical doctor and is an individual who heals or influences healing. The first physician licensing laws were passed in the 1870s by the states in order to stem what was viewed by physicians as uncontrolled access to the market. By 1881, half of the states had physician licensure, although serious enforcement did not begin until the 1890s (Baker 1984). Under the new regulations, unlicensed medical practice was to be punished by fine or imprisonment. The publication of the *Flexner Report* in 1910, sponsored by the American Medical Association (AMA), eventually led to AMA control of medical education and regulation of physicians and auxiliary workers (Flexner 1910).[3] The report argued for higher levels of education and greater control of the medical profession by doctors. It also recommended that the number of openings in medical school be limited. One of the main consequences of the rise of physician licensing is that medical doctors are now required to pass additional exams after graduation from medical school and do residencies to become licensed physicians. A key issue is that licensure endows physicians with considerable control over what services and work tasks nonphysicians are allowed to perform under state law or administrative rules established by state administrative boards. The *Flexner Report* resulted in the AMA's gaining de facto control of licensing and regulation of physicians across all states through the Federation of State Medical Boards (Beck 2004). The number of physicians relative to the population declined by 15 percent over the next 30-year period following the report, leading to substantial gains in physicians' earnings.

In an analysis of the impact of these restrictions on wage determination for doctors, Milton Friedman and Simon Kuznets, who each won the Nobel Prize in economics, noted the large impact of the AMA on enhancing the earnings of doctors following the *Flexner Report* (Friedman and Kuznets 1945). For example, the authors make the argument that the difference in ease of entry reflects a deliberate policy to limit the total number of physicians to prevent so-called overcrowding of the profession. Friedman and Kuznets attribute the deliberate restrictions of supply to the AMA and its Council on Medical Education—a claim that invited much criticism from the AMA (Friedman and Friedman 1998). The authors estimate that as much as 17 percent of the excess of mean income in medicine is due to these restrictions on general labor supply conditions for physicians.

In a subsequent book, *Capitalism and Freedom*, Friedman (1962) argues that doctors believe they need to control the supply of physicians, and that if the supply of doctors becomes too large, their earnings will fall. As a consequence, doctors claim that they will prescribe too many procedures in order to achieve their desired or expected income, and that they need that level of income in order to behave ethically. In other occupations that do not have this ability to control supply, this type of behavior would be viewed as unacceptable or illegal. Friedman states that the more plausible rationale for licensing for physicians—such as the ability to detect contagious diseases by a well-trained doctor—is important but rarely used by the profession. Moreover, the ability to eliminate unethical or unscrupulous members of any occupation is rarely used. In addition, the ability to have many alternative forms of medical care is limited by occupational licensing provisions. Forms of medicine that are not provided by physicians and that the medical establishment finds inappropriate were restricted through occupational licensure statutes or administrative procedures. For example, the *Flexner Report* forbade chiropractors from being considered medical practitioners.

A noted in Chapter 1, a key argument in the political economy approach for licensing is the term the *Cadillac effect*. As presented in *Capitalism and Freedom* (Friedman 1962), licensing standards are set so high that only upper-income individuals can purchase the service. Lower-quality services are forbidden under the police powers of the state. Since licensing provides state-sanctioned monopolies, and those in the occupation can set the standard, the entry barrier is set high. In tying this analogy to the car market, if only expensive Cadillacs are allowed to be purchased or driven, and less expensive models, such as Fords and Chevys, are forbidden, then the consequence for the service market is that the consumer receives a very high-quality service or nothing at all. The use of substitutes—such as, for example, nurse practitioners for physicians or dental hygienists for dentists—is forbidden or restricted by efforts from the physicians' and dentists' lobbies in the legislature (Kleiner et al. 2014). Moreover, Friedman (1962) also said that these practices reduce innovation, because new techniques or procedures are not allowed by law or administrative statements from the licensing board. More recently, restrictions have occurred because of a limitation on the number of medical residencies that are required to become a licensed physician (Benson et al. 2014). This has had a particularly negative impact on physicians from other countries who are applying to become physicians in the United States, and it has resulted in a reduction in the quantity of physicians.

Mortgage Brokers

Mortgage brokers are intermediaries who both match potential mortgage borrowers and lenders and assist them in completing the loan origination process for the purpose of purchasing property. Brokers have typically operated as independent service providers, not as agents or employees of either borrowers or lenders, and they are compensated by fees paid by the borrower and sometimes the lender as well. A little more than three decades ago, the mortgage industry was made up almost entirely of large integrated firms (banks and savings and loans), which managed the entire process of bringing borrowers and investors together. They located investors and borrowers, recommended the appropriate type of loan, investigated and analyzed borrowers' credit worthiness and the value of their collateral, closed the loans, serviced the loans, and made payments to the investors (Jacobides 2005). Mortgage broker businesses are generally small, with approximately 83 percent of companies licensed in only one state and employ between one and five mortgage loan originators. Additionally, 87 percent of these companies have only a single location. With deregulation and technological change in the home loan industry during the 1990s, the lending process became vertically integrated so that mortgage brokers found borrowers and worked with them to apply for an appropriate loan; mortgage banks evaluated applications and funded them, and sometimes serviced loans. They also bundled them and sold them as securities (Jacobides 2005). Brokers also sometimes initially fund loans and resell them.

Several factors have led to changes in the mortgage industry, including the rise of mortgage brokers. With the deregulation of the industry, there was a large proliferation in mortgage products available to subprime markets, which are more risky investments, and the increased emphasis on volume worked together to penetrate higher-risk markets that had previously been ignored by the industry. Between 1993 and 2001, subprime lenders' share of the home purchase lending market grew from 1 percent to 6 percent. In lower-income households, the subprime share was 10 percent. Also, in lower-income households, subprime refinance loans made up 27 percent of home refinance loans, a growth of more than 400 percent during this same period (Apgar, Bendimerad, and Essene 2007).

Since this is a largely new occupation, its regulation began in the states only in the early 1990s. In a data collection effort and evaluation of the rigor of the regulations covering mortgage brokers, Pahl (2007) notes that they more than doubled from 1996 to 2005. Further, the key factor in the regulation of the occupation is a bonding requirement.[4] When brokers are required to have a bond of $50,000, for example, this typically means that they pay an annual premium, ranging from several hundred to a few thousand dollars, to a surety bond company. It does not mean that the broker must own and place in trust a fixed-income security with a market value of $50,000. Under specified conditions of broker nonperformance of duties spelled out in the governing laws and regulations, third parties, such as the broker's customers, may collect up to the amount of the bond from the surety company. The role of the surety company is to ensure that a valid claim will be promptly paid.[5] If this occurs, the surety company will seek full compensation from the broker for the amount it paid out to the third party, plus expenses. The broker's annual premium or the basis of his or her salary is thus a fee paid to guarantee a line of contingent credit up to a legally required amount. In setting the annual premium it charges a broker, a surety company considers both the expected value of claims against the broker and the probability of collecting from the broker for any amounts paid out. Consequently, the bond company may conduct detailed screening of applicants, similar to credit underwriting, before issuing the bond.

An analysis of the influence of having a stringent bonding requirement shows that tighter bonding/net worth requirements are also associated with lower volumes of loans processed and a higher percentage of high-priced loans originated. The results from Kleiner and Todd (2009) show that the relationship between mortgage broker licensing and market outcomes differs among the types of licensing requirements. Specifically, financial bonding or net worth requirements are associated with somewhat higher earnings; modest reductions in the number of mortgage brokers and the number of subprime loans originated, as well as with somewhat higher foreclosure rates; and higher interest rates on brokered loans. The evolution of regulation in this industry has had numerous unintended side effects for workers in the occupation, who now receive higher pay, and for the consumers of their financial services, who have fewer brokers and greater constraints on their ability to compete on price and on their availability (Kleiner and Todd 2009).

Interior Designers

The Bureau of Labor Statistics' (BLS) *Occupational Outlook Handbook* provides a definition of the occupation of interior designers: "Interior designers draw upon many disciplines to enhance the function, safety, and aesthetics of interior spaces. Their main concerns are with how different colors, textures, furniture, lighting, and space work together to meet the needs of a building's occupants. Designers plan interior spaces of almost every type of building, including offices, airport terminals, theaters, shopping malls, restaurants, hotels, schools, hospitals, and private residences" (BLS 2012, p. 314).

The work of interior designers overlaps and competes with that of engineers, architects, and other construction workers. The fear of remaining unregulated among these occupations that are governmentally regulated in all states is captured in the following statement by the American Society of Interior Designers on its website: "It is no secret that some other professional groups would like to limit, control, or even eliminate the practice of interior design as a unique profession. It would be naive to believe that they are not making their cases."[6]

The interior design occupation is a relatively recent addition to the purview of governmental oversight. The professional association for the occupation, the American Institute of Interior Designers (AIID), was founded in 1931; it was not until the postwar period in the 1950s that the organization had grown and sought to become regulated (ASID 2005). In 1968, voluntary certification began through ASID, the successor organization that was designed to pave the way for licensing. The professional organization also began to work with interior design programs to strengthen curriculums and develop continuing education programs for the members of the occupation. In the following decade, AIID and another interior design organization merged to form ASID and were immediately assigned the task of collecting information on state regulations for the profession (ASID 2005). In the 1980s the association began encouraging state-by-state registration regulations, and they signed an accord with the architects' professional association to support only certification, or what became known within the occupation as title acts. The agreement allowed architects to register interior designers in states with these acts and establish joint regulatory boards. Within this context, the agreement gave interior designers with expertise in the field the ability to use this title, and those persons who did not fulfill the qualifications were forbidden from using the terms *registered* or *certified*. In 1999, however, the ASID board voted to withdraw from the accord and aggressively pursue full occupational licensing by the states, which became known as practice acts.

When government regulation of engineers evolved to include civil, electrical, mechanical, and industrial by the 1960s, the law stated that only engineers can sign off on initial and final construction design and implementation. As a result, interior designers were relegated to an inferior position within the construction industry. Moreover, architects were held responsible for the development of the initial design of structures, which further diminished the role of interior designers in the eyes of the law. More generally, state and local governments have gradually assumed a more important role in determining how work is to be done in construction. The appropriate types of labor inputs in construction are determined only through governmental statutes or administrative procedures. Working within the constraints of this institutional environment, interior designers concluded that the only way to obtain access to certain types of work in this field was to take steps to become a regulated occupation. With this in mind, they pushed for licensing in several states. However, they have had limited success—they have obtained full licensure in only three states plus the District of Columbia.

Overall, interior designers are lobbying government on a regular basis to become licensed or to obtain what is called a practice act. In part because of push back by developers, unregulated designers, and consumer groups, this occupation is having a difficult time breaking out of the small number of states that have licensed its members, and Alabama's Supreme Court deregulated interior designers based on insufficient evidence that it posed a threat to health and safety. As background, the state implemented a practice act in 2001, which was then ruled unconstitutional in 2007 by the state supreme court. If a practice act increases wages for interior designers, we would then expect to see a substantial increase in wages between 2002 and 2007 in Alabama. For example, interior designers in Alabama saw a wage increase of 46 percent under a practice act. By comparison, the national mean wage increased 17 percent over the same period of time (Alexander et al. 2009). These gains explain why the members of ASID continue to push for legislation to regulate the occupation.

SUMMARY AND CONCLUSIONS

Specialized workers have long attempted to limit competition and set standards for entry into an occupation. Friedman (1962) notes that the process can be traced to the time of ancient Greece and the Hippocratic Oath, and that it puts limits on entry into medicine. Also, there are many similarities between unions and occupational licensing. In medieval times, guilds also attempted to limit entry into occupations with the help of local political leaders. The movement from a nation of shopkeepers and small firms operating in local labor markets to the Industrial Revolution resulted in a decline in the system of guilds, as manufacturing firms largely trained workers for specific jobs that were required for large assembly line tasks, but with little need for the government to set standards. With more growth in the service economy, workers in the service sector have formed associations that lobby the state legislatures and governors in the United States.

The outcome has been growth in the regulated sector of the labor market. Physicians, mortgage brokers, and interior designers are at different stages of occupational regulation and licensure. In the case of physicians, the occupation has been able to largely control the market for new doctors since the early twentieth century. Mortgage brokers have been captive to large swings in the housing market. It is an emerging occupation that has seen state-level regulations, such as the required bonding of practitioners, and an influence on wages and prices for the consumers of their services.

Finally, interior designers have been trying to get on equal footing with engineers and architects by seeking state-by-state licensing. Thus far they have had only modest success in achieving full licensing in the United States. In general, interior designers have promoted occupational licensing with much less input by the public. In addition, this curious standard-setting legal institution seems to behave differently in different occupations and is similar to guilds because they had different tactics in different countries and across varying industries and towns. "To paraphrase Tolstoy, all unlicensed occupations are alike; each licensed occupation is licensed in its own way."[7]

Notes

1. For a link to the entire program, see http://vimeo.com/26912276 (accessed July 7, 2015).
2. The Taft-Hartley amendments to the act do, however, allow for unions to be voted out, and in right-to-work states, individuals do not have to join a union or pay union dues. When a union wins an election at an establishment, it is the exclusive representative of the workers for a minimum of one year.
3. This policy of giving control of regulation to an association has occurred in a number of occupations. For example, physical therapists boards

have largely followed the directives of the association in increasing the requirements of newly licensed physical therapists to a doctoral degree.
4. For background on the market for surety bonds in general and mortgage broker surety bonds in particular, see www.jwsuretybonds.com (accessed July 14, 2015).
5. Surety companies investigate the validity of claims before paying out. We are referring here to claims they consider valid.
6. See http://asidcanv.org/students/student-legislative-resources/ (accessed July 14, 2015).
7. Charles Wheelan, from the Harris School of Public Policy at the University of Chicago, used this statement in a blurb he wrote for my book *Stages of Occupational Regulation: Analysis of Case Studies* (Upjohn Institute 2013).

Chapter 3

The Costs, Mobility, and Quality of Occupational Licensing Services

> *Determining the desirability of government intervention therefore requires a careful assessment of the costs of imperfect markets relative to the costs and benefits of imperfect regulation, with full recognition of the inevitable shortcomings in each.*
> —Nancy Rose (2014, p. 21)

Occupational licensing is a growing labor market institution in the United States. For example, during the 2012–2013 legislative sessions, at least seven new occupations were licensed, ranging from scrap metal recyclers in Louisiana, therapeutic shoe fitters in Alabama, to body artists in the District of Columbia. On the other hand, during the same time period, three governors (from Idaho, Iowa, and Indiana) vetoed legislation from their own party's dominated legislature that would have licensed several new occupations (Associated Press 2013; Branstad 2013; Reynolds 2015).

What might be the aggregate costs of licensing in the U.S. economy? One measure of an upper bound can be calculated as follows. There are approximately 38 million licensed workers, with average annual earnings of about $41,000 in 2010. Using a standard economic model, at the high end of the estimates of the impact, occupational licensing can result in 2.8 million fewer jobs with an annual cost to consumers of $203 billion (Kleiner 2015; Kleiner, Krueger, and Mas 2011). This amount is a transfer of income from consumers to licensed workers. If consumers are middle-income individuals, and licensed workers are well above average, this could result in a reallocation of resources from middle-income to higher-income practitioners. In addition, there would be lost output as well as potential misallocation effects from the misuse of labor resources related to these government-mandated regulations (Schmidt 2012). The costs could include using government-mandated labor resources relative to economically efficient inputs in the production of labor services (Kleiner 2013).[1]

Without doing a detailed analysis at the occupation-by-occupation and state, county, or national level, it is difficult to say which occupations can be justified based on quality considerations, though when studies have been conducted they have found a number of cases where occupational licensing reduces employment and increases prices but does not result in better services (Kleiner 2013). For example, Kleiner and Kudrle (2000) find that tougher occupational licensing of dentists does not lead to improved measured dental outcomes of patients, but it results in higher prices of certain services, likely because there are fewer dentists.[2]

Overall, current analytical research shows few significant benefits of occupational regulation for consumers and no major effect on the quality of service received by consumers or on the demand for the service, other than through potential price effects.

As was noted in Chapter 2, there was little occupational licensing throughout much of the nineteenth century (Langford 2009). The licensing of occupations in the United States has evolved mainly at the state level. As mentioned earlier, the major Supreme Court case that established the right of states to grant licenses was the *Dent v. West Virginia 129 U.S. 114* decision in 1889. The decision established state law as the appropriate venue to deal with protecting the health, welfare, or safety of citizens. There was a steady increase in the regulation of occupations in the United States, with 30 occupations licensed in 1920, including more than 2,800 statutory provisions in the different states (Greene 1969). At the beginning of the twentieth century, occupations such as doctors, dentists, and lawyers attained full licensure in most states. The duration of how long an occupation has been licensed often is a good indicator to how economically successful the occupation has become over time (Han and Kleiner 2015).

With new information technology, consumers who use companies like Uber have the ability to directly contact suppliers of these services, and they have lots of information about the driver. As a result, the value of occupational licenses has been questioned. Uber, an app-based transportation network, serves as a taxi company. The company provides transportation services without the benefit of a typical occupational license. Customers and drivers rate each other immediately after a trip, and this information is shared with new potential customers and drivers. The drivers, who function as independent contractors, are vetted through the company and have private driver's licenses, but unlike most cab drivers they are not required to have a taxi or chauffeur's license through the state, county, or city. Consequently, they do not pay these licensing fees to the government, and Uber is not subject to other regulations of taxis, such as metered fares and guaranteed coverage of certain destinations. Many customers seem to enjoy the benefits of competition with conventional cabs, such as the chance of lower prices, and in some cities Uber drivers almost serve as the family chauffeur (Kapp 2014). On the other hand, taxi companies and drivers and government officials have expressed public safety concerns about Uber's lack of regulation, with some cities, such as Portland, Oregon, attempting to ban Uber drivers in the city. The fate of Uber and similar services, even as they continue to grow, will likely be determined through the courts and, potentially, legislation.

Unfortunately, it is difficult to ascertain what share of the workforce requires a license to do their jobs or how this varies across states, since this information has not been tracked in government surveys. In 2013, however, Harris Poll Interactive, in a project for the Institute for Justice funded by the Templeton Foundation, conducted such a survey of approximately 10,000 workers that had been patterned on earlier smaller-scale surveys (Kleiner and Krueger 2013; Kleiner and Vorotnikov 2015). The Harris Poll found that 28.43 percent of the respondents answered that they were either licensed or certified. Approximately 6.75 percent said that individuals who did not have a license could do the work, which is the definition of government certification. Another 1.79 percent said that all who worked would eventually be required to be certified or licensed, bringing the total that are or eventually must be licensed or certified by government to 30.22 percent.[3] Table 3.1 shows the education, testing, and internship requirements for those facing licensing or certification.

These huge variations in licensing requirements across states often have little relationship to the ability of the individuals to do the tasks related to the occupation. The use of licensing varies for the same occupation. For example, only 7 states license dental assistants, and 13 states license locksmiths. Iowa requires 490 days to become a licensed cosmetologist, but the national average is 372 days, and New York and Massachusetts require only 233 days (Carpenter et al. 2012). In addition, occupational licensing is often not tied to issues of clear health and safety concerns at the point of service. To illustrate, Michigan requires 1,460 days to become an athletic trainer but only 26 days to be licensed as an emergency medical technician. These examples provide some illustrations of the variance in training licensed workers across states and licensing occupations within states. However, there does not appear to be a rational approach in terms of the health and safety of the public—which is the primary stated purpose of this kind of regulation—regarding why some occupations are licensed and oth-

Table 3.1 Percentage of Workers Who Require Specific Education and Testing to Become Licensed or Certified

	Licensed workers facing requirement	Certified workers facing requirement
High school diploma	75.1	66.6
College degree	47.7	28.5
Pass an exam	88.9	85.9
Performance test	67.8	61.1
Continuing education	67.8	52.9
Internship	46.5	35.3
License/certificate renewal test	34.5	33.9

SOURCE: Kleiner and Vorotnikov (2015). Harris conducted the survey in early and mid-2013. Individuals aged 18 or older who were in the labor force were eligible for the survey. A total of 9,850 individuals were interviewed. Kleiner and Vorotnikov limit their analysis to those who were at the time of the survey employed or had a job during the previous 12 months.

ers are not, and why some require long training programs and exams while others require relatively little time in the classroom. Although these differences may in part reflect the industry and human capital characteristics of the state, they may also reflect the ability of occupational associations to get licensing for many more of their workers. Figure 3.1 shows a map of the number of states that license various occupations by high, medium, and low. For example, Iowa has twice the percentage of licensed workers as Rhode Island, New Hampshire, or Indiana. Does the huge variation in the occupational regulation system shown in Figure 3.1 reflect the equity and efficiency trade-offs of this type of regulation? Beyond the characteristics of the state, the industry composition of the state may help determine the percent of the workforce that is licensed. Nevertheless, the state-specific political forces may also be an important factor in the large variation in the number of workers who have attained an occupational license.

Figure 3.1 Share of Workforce Licensed, by State (%)

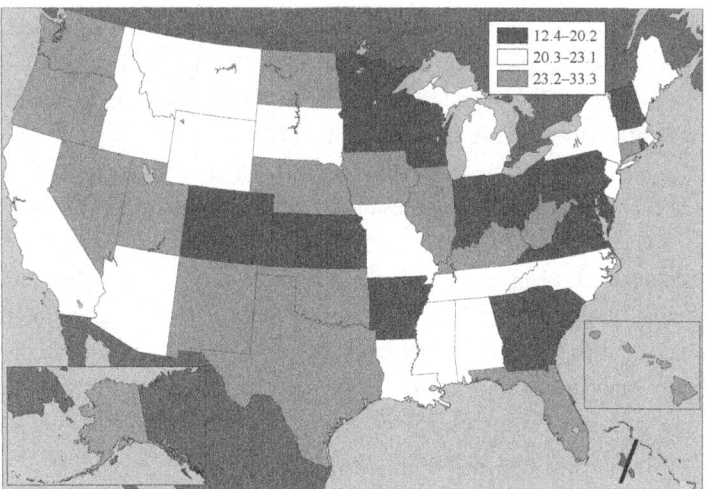

NOTE: The three categories were constructed to contain roughly the same number of states.
SOURCE: Kleiner and Vorotnikov (2015) based on an analysis of data from a Harris poll of 9,850 individuals conducted in the first half of 2013.

INFLUENCE ON WAGES AND EMPLOYMENT

The impact of being in a licensed occupation on the hourly earnings of universally regulated occupations relative to similar unlicensed individuals has recently seen considerable research and analysis. For the occupations examined in the literature, being in a licensed occupation appears to increase earnings by 10–15 percent, which is at the lower bound of the impact of other labor market institutions, such as unions (Kleiner and Krueger 2010, 2013). For individuals whose occupations are licensed in some states and not in others, the impact of being licensed is much smaller, about 5–8 percent (Gittleman, Klee, and Kleiner 2015; Gittleman and Kleiner, forthcoming; Kleiner 2006).

Licensing generally increases the economic status of practitioners (Gittleman, Klee, and Kleiner 2015). Policymakers need to examine whether this is either a result of increased quality caused by greater training and higher quality services or a consequence of restricting competition by limiting entry into the occupations, or both. In addition, the evidence using federal government surveys suggests that the benefits of licensing are mainly for individuals who are relatively well off (Gittleman, Klee, and Kleiner 2015).

A study of occupational laws for 10 major licensed occupations in the U.S. labor market estimates the influence of time from the passage of a law to its influence in the labor market. Time from the passage of occupational licensing laws, called duration, is important when analyzing occupational licensing because states often enact "grandfather clauses" that protect existing workers, and new workers have higher entry standards than existing workers, thus increasing the costs to new entrants. This process limits the supply of labor, and those in the occupation can gain economic rents. Using historical data on the year that an occupation was licensed by a state and the data available from the American Community Survey and the Current Population Survey from 1950 to 2010, Han and Kleiner (2015) develop estimates of the impact of licensing duration on wages. Their estimates suggest that it takes at least 10 years to realize the full economic wage effects of occupational licensing. There is considerable variation in the effects of regulation. For the higher-education and higher-income occupations working mainly in the quasi-private sector, such as physicians, dentists, and lawyers, licensing appears to have large effects through either limiting entry or restricting movement between the states. However, for occupations such as teachers, nurses, and cosmetologists, the impact of licensing on earnings is murky, with some studies finding small effects and others finding none (Kleiner 2006, 2013). However, for teachers and nurses, licensing reduces interstate migration (Johnson and Kleiner 2015). The influence of licensing on employment growth is more gradual, but the findings suggest that licensed occupations grow more slowly in states that license than in those that do not (Kleiner 2006).

INFLUENCE ON GEOGRAPHIC MOBILITY

In the last 20 years, occupational licensing has been moving in the opposite direction relative to gross interstate migration (Johnson and Kleiner 2015). Figure 3.2 shows that beginning in the mid-1980s, interstate migration started to decline as the percent of the workforce that have occupational licenses continued to grow. Several studies have documented the general decline of Americans' movement across states. To explain the decline, these studies often use models that include improved information by migrants of job opportunities, cost of living, and other amenities. Consequently, there is less return migration and cross-state movement because information in the labor market is much better than in the past. The primary reason for this improvement is the growth of the Internet and information available to potential movers. Despite its steep downward trend, migration within the United States remains higher than that within most other developed countries (Kaplan and Schulhofer-Wohl 2012; Molloy, Smith, and Wozniak 2011). However, recent empirical evidence sug-

Figure 3.2 Occupational Licensing and Interstate Migration, 1950–2008

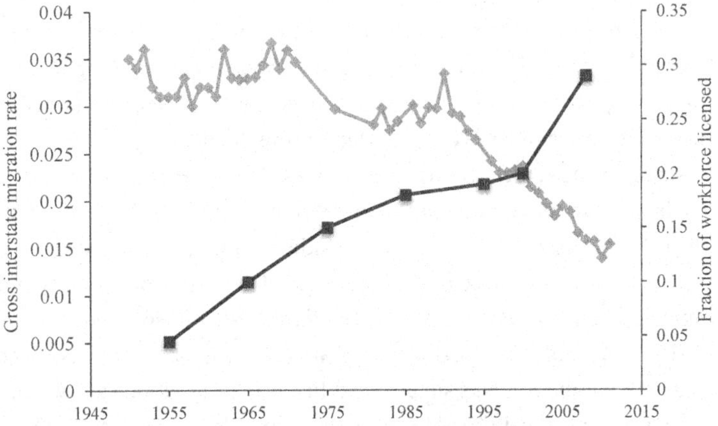

[Chart: Left axis "Gross interstate migration rate" (0 to 0.04) with a declining series from ~0.035 in the late 1940s to ~0.015 by 2008; Right axis "Fraction of workforce licensed" (0 to 0.35) with a rising series from ~0.05 in 1955 to ~0.33 by 2008. X-axis years 1945–2015.]

SOURCE: Johnson and Kleiner (2015).

gests that occupational licensing has contributed to this decline and has produced the following results: workers not being able to take jobs that they want without significantly higher regulatory administrative costs, and consumers not being able to take advantage of more services at the lowest cost in rapidly growing areas (Moretti 2012). This has become a particularly important issue for military families, who are often moved across state lines—10 times more than the average American. If the trailing partner is licensed, he or she must spend a considerable amount of time and money to seek reaccreditation (U.S. Executive Office of the President 2013, 2015).

Occupational licensing can deter geographical movements in several ways. First, under licensing statutes and administrative processes, investments for entry into an occupation are more difficult (especially in the absence of reciprocity, which are agreements among states to accept each other's practitioners). The requirements commonly involve qualification criteria, passing exams, and in many cases, the engagement in continuing professional development activities (an investment that continues throughout one's career). Second, in many professional labor markets, practicing the occupation also involves location-specific investments, such as developing social capital in local reputation, an additional cost that the worker has to bear if he or she decides to migrate (Pashigian 1979, 1980). Finally, if a worker in a particular licensed occupation moves from a highly regulated labor market to a less regulated one, there is the possibility of a wage penalty if the wage premium associated with licensing is higher in the home state compared to that in the destination. As a result, one would expect licensing to add to the cost of mobility and to be inversely related to labor movements. However, to the extent that educational and other regulation-related requirements are harmonized, individuals would move to take advantage of economic opportunities (e.g., in the form of a wage premium). Further, the ease with which one can access information on entry to the profession (e.g., procedures to follow for recognition of qualifications and residency requirements) also is likely to reduce the cost of movement that is taken on by the individual. Conversely, tougher licensing in the host state would deter outmigration because it is unlikely that individuals in occupations that are more heavily regulated in a state are likely to receive a wage offer that is high enough to encourage movement out of those states.

Within this model, occupational licensing has been cited as a policy that not only may distort the operation of labor markets (Friedman 1962; Rottenberg 1980) but also may act as a deterrent to labor mobility. Holen (1965) is among the first policy studies to analyze the effects of U.S. state licensing arrangements and practices in the health care professions, focusing on interstate mobility and the allocation of professional labor resources. The author finds that the empirical evidence is consistent with the view that professional licensing arrangements and practices in dentistry and law restrict interstate mobility among dentists and lawyers and distort the allocation of professional personnel in these fields. Follow-up work along the same lines by Pashigian

(1979) shows that occupational licensing reduces the mobility of individuals across state lines. Kleiner, Gay, and Greene (1982) find that restrictive licensing may operate as a barrier to mobility, causing a misallocation of labor resources across states, with increased earnings for the practitioners in those states with the most restrictive barriers.

Reexamining the issue with more current data, Tenn (2001) finds that supply restrictions cause equilibrium wages to rise because of these supply changes, which results in higher-quality workers with presumably higher wages. Drawing on prior research by Pashigian (1979) and Kleiner, Gay, and Greene (1982), Tenn examines the influence of licensing for attorneys, an occupation that has long been licensed in the United States. He finds that migration rates and licensing statutes jointly have significant influence in explaining wages and concludes that both these issues need to be addressed as part of the analysis of the impact of occupational licensing.

Federman, Harrington, and Krynski (2006) also examine issues for lower-income practitioners who are covered by licensing laws. The authors estimate the effects of licensing regulations on the entry of manicurist immigrants into the occupation. Their findings show that the level of migration is impeded by the existence and restrictiveness (in terms of minimum entry standards) of state licensing regulations. In particular, they estimate that the requirement to have an additional 100 hours of training reduces the likelihood of having a Vietnamese manicurist by 4.5 percent, while states requiring some level of English proficiency were 5.7 percentage points less likely to have a Vietnamese manicurist. Consequently, policies that affect migration are not limited to just high-income individuals.

Taken together, these studies support the view that regulation may limit the number of practitioners in a nation and that a policy of reducing barriers to interstate migration would provide benefits to workers and consumers. If this is the case, then nationwide endorsement through policies that do not limit entry requirements could alleviate uneven geographic distribution of licensed practitioners and ease possible location-specific mismatches. Second, nationwide endorsement, which is the acceptance of the credentials of those from another state, represents a potential policy reform since the proposal is often supported by a majority of the members of a profession relative to deregulation. The ability to move across state lines and legally work would allow individuals to more easily go where there are jobs with fewer impediments for movement across state lines. This is particularly important since the growth in wage variation across geographic areas may make it more advantageous to move across state lines (Moretti 2012). Finally, barriers to interstate migration may not allow labor markets to function in their most efficient manner.

INFLUENCE ON PRICES

The practices that raise wages and prices include restrictions on interstate mobility, advertising, and other commercial practices (Bond et al. 1980; Feldman and Begun 1978; Shepard 1978). The impact of licensing-related practices on prices ranges from 5 to 33 percent, depending on the type of occupational practice and location (Kleiner 2006).[4] For example, the influence of the lack of reciprocity in dentistry raises prices by 15 percent (Shepard 1978). Restrictions on the number of hygienists that a dentist may employ increase the average price of a dental visit by 7 percent (Liang and Ogur 1987). Restrictions on nurse practitioners' tasks relative to physicians' raise prices of well-child exams by 10 percent (Kleiner et al. 2014). If the price of a well-child exam is approximately $100, and there were approximately 60,000,000 medical visits in 2012, then the potential cost savings of relaxing these licensing requirements could result in approximately $600,000,000 per year for just this one medical procedure (Kleiner et al. 2014).

OCCUPATIONAL LICENSING AS SOCIAL INSURANCE

The rationale for these effects on prices could be that government regulations reduce uncertainty or the likelihood of poor service, or "lemons," in the market (Akerlof 1970). A review of the body of theory from experimental economics and psychology shows that consumers value the reduction in downside risk more than they value the benefits of a positive outcome (Kahneman, Knetsch, and Thaler 1991). This consumer preference for reducing the risk of a highly negative outcome has been called "loss aversion," which is an element of the "prospect theory" developed by Kahneman and Tversky (1979). For example, social welfare may be increased substantially by minimizing the likelihood of a poor diagnosis as a consequence of going to an incompetent physician, because the incompetent physicians have been weeded out as a result of the monitoring effects of licensing. Consequently, occupational licensing may also reduce patients' perceived benefits of receiving nonstandard but potentially highly effective treatment from an unlicensed practitioner of nontraditional medicine. Using the power of the state to both limit the downside risk of poor quality care and reduce the possibility of an upside benefit may be a trade-off that maximizes consumer utility or welfare. Evidence of the acceptance of this trade-off can be found in the growth of occupational licensing in many countries during the past century (Kleiner 2006). To an extent, according to Kahneman and Tversky, licensing could be perceived as a form of social insurance that costs consumers more because it protects them against potential downside losses.

As a consequence, consumers perceive the service to be of higher quality because of licensing, and they demand more of the service, which drives up the price. On the other hand, regulations could be a way for current practitioners, by limiting entry or restricting information on prices in the market for the service, to raise their own wages (Friedman 1962; Kleiner 2015). If government grants a monopoly in the market for the service, the long-term impact would be lower-quality services, a misallocation of resources, and higher prices. From the empirical studies of licensing, it is difficult to tell which of these effects dominates in the determination of price increases for licensed services. However, a consequence for regulated occupations with high incomes, such dentists and lawyers, is the ability to raise prices through the impacts of regulation, restricting the supply of practitioners and controlling the allocation of work to them relative to unregulated workers within the industry. The monopoly power granted and enforced by the state may shift income from lower-income customers to higher-income practitioners, which may contribute to greater income inequality.

An alternative explanation for these price increases that is often given by the occupations' professional associations is that the method of delivering services for the profession has changed over time, and that allowing a group of experts to supervise, govern, and recommend changes would standardize the practices and reduce uncertainty in the minds of consumers. In the Supreme Court case *North Carolina State Board of Dental Examiners v. Federal Trade Commission* (2014), argued in October 2014 and decided in February 2015 in favor of the Federal Trade Commission, it was suggested that when members of the profession are on the licensing board, they attempt to capture work from other occupations. In this case it was the work of unlicensed teeth whiteners who were working in malls and spas selling teeth whitening products. The dental licensing board of North Carolina claimed that individuals who were not dentists and sold over-the-counter teeth whitening kits were practicing dentistry without an occupational license. When the dental board sent cease-and-desist letters to the mall vendors, the Federal Trade Commission viewed such an action as a violation of the Sherman Antitrust Act. In the oral arguments at the Supreme Court, Associate Justice Breyer expressed concern about bureaucrats making decisions in areas where only trained professionals are knowledgeable and have competence in making appropriate decisions (Liptak 2014). Although a regulatory board consists of licensed practitioners who possess specific knowledge of the tasks needed to perform the job, it can lead to perverse incentives in which the interests of the practitioners are in conflict with the interests of the public. In North Carolina, six of the eight board members were practicing dentists and elected by other practicing dentists, not chosen by the governor, legislature, or other officials responsible to the public. While the dentists have an interest in exclusively reserving the right to sell a profitable service, the public has an interest in having access to a sufficient number of individuals to do the job at a reasonable price and at an acceptable level of quality. This Supreme Court case illustrates how occupational regulation can lead to conflicts over who can legally provide services to the public. In this case it was the relatively well-off dentists taking work and income from relatively lower-income sales representatives of teeth whitening products and services.

As the price of dental services goes up, so does average quality per practitioner, which is seen in higher-quality services as reflected in higher prices. By having better dentists through more training, the patient is likely to receive better care but at a higher price. Further, capital expenditures, through more sophisticated and expensive equipment, have increased the required return on investment for either a sole practitioner or for a large provider of medical services (Cutler and Berndt 2001). On the other hand, standardization through occupational licensing may also stifle innovation or new techniques of practice by the licensing board by not allowing new procedures or competitors to be introduced.

INFLUENCE ON QUALITY OF SERVICES

Many studies have attempted to develop methods to estimate the influence of licensing on quality or the demand for licensed services. On this issue there are a disproportionate number of studies on regulation in dentistry, in part because for many years dentistry had large variations in state licensing requirements (Shepard 1978). Moreover, outcome measures like cavities were easy to identify and quantify. Dollar values across political jurisdictions were generally available. For example, Holen (1978) finds that licensing reduces the likelihood of adverse outcomes and increases the quality of care, but Carroll and Gaston (1981) and Kleiner and Kudrle (2000) find no effect. Since Holen and Carrol and Gaston use the same data source gathered from the Naval recruits, the differences in the outcomes rely largely on different measures of outcomes. Holen uses a measure of the condition of the teeth itself, such as cavities or broken or chipped teeth. On the other hand, Carroll and Gaston use measures of an oral hygiene index, which focuses on the soft tissue and includes measures such as gum disease. Kleiner and Kudrle use measures of dental health that incorporate Holen's measure, as well as those by Carrol and Gaston, and they use a "quality-adjusted" pass rate as well as statutory factors in each state. Kleiner and Kudrle's analysis uses a broader number of controls for economic and demographic factors. With these updated and more refined measures of dental condition, the characteristics of the individuals in the study, and measures of regulation by the states, they find no impact of tougher state licensing laws and administrative procedures on measures of dental condition. This suggests that occupational licensing generally has little to no effect on outcomes, even using point of service delivery.

Studies of other occupations, from construction contractors to teachers, suggest that tougher forms of regulation have murky effects on quality or the demand for the service (Angrist and Guryan 2003; Kleiner and Petree 1988; Maurizi 1980; Shapiro 1986). For contractors, Maurizi finds that allowing lower-quality contractors to obtain licenses would reduce the quality-enhancing impacts of this type of labor market regulation. In education, the growth of occupational licensing over the past two decades has resulted in uncertain effects on student test scores, a generally recognized measure of quality in education. Carroll and Gaston (1981), in the case studies for seven widely varying licensed occupations, find that licensing has either a negative or no impact on the quality of services received by consumers. In another study on physicians, Paul (1982) states that "licensing legislation was the result of organized physicians employing the political system for limiting entry and the concomitant increasing of return to incumbent medical practitioners" (p. 27). However, using a theoretical model of the impacts of licensing, Shapiro argues that licensing should be thought of by income segments of the consumer market for licensed services. The argument is that wealthier consumers who value quality more highly gain the benefits, but lower-income individuals with lesser relative demand for quality services would lose from tougher licensing standards by having less access to the service (Kleiner and Kudrle 2000; Shapiro 1986).

Another factor in the growth of the demand for licensing is its disproportionate prevalence in medical service delivery, an industry that has been growing rapidly with an aging population. Consumption of medical services grew 25 percent as a percentage of all consumer purchases from 1984 to 1995 (Ford and Ginsburg 2001). Moreover, the prices of medical services have risen more rapidly than overall prices in the economy (Triplett 2001), and about 76 percent of nonphysican services include individuals who have a license (Kleiner et al. 2014). An important factor in the growth of this sector has been that technological change has grown much more rapidly in the medical industry than in other services in the economy, which has led to the need for more standardized labor inputs (Fixler and Ginsburg 2001). Licensing may have fulfilled this demand for a minimum requirement of standardization as a complimentary input to the rapid technological change in this industry.

In one of the few field studies of the impacts of licensing on quality, the Federal Trade Commission examined the relationship between licensing and the overuse of services (Phelan 1974). In this study, televisions with known defects were used to determine the incidents of oversubscribed services in three locations: 1) Washington, D.C., which did not require a license for television repair; 2) New Orleans, Louisiana, which licenses the individuals; and 3) San Francisco, California, which licenses the facility but not the individual. One of the findings was that the Louisiana licensing law does not protect the consumer from what has been defined as "parts fraud" (Phelan 1974). The estimates from the study found that parts fraud was about 20 percent in San Francisco, compared to about 50 percent in New Orleans and Washington, D.C. Therefore, licensing individuals may not be an optimal method of consumer protection relative to no licensing or regulating a business. Although policymakers may wish occupational licensing to be a method of enhancing quality, there is little evidence to support this assumption for consumers, even at point of sale. If, however, licensing reduces the worst outcomes, such as a furnace exploding because a licensed boilermaker had the training to detect the problem, then the regulations may be perceived as insurance that reduces downside risks (Kahneman and Tversky 1979).

In a field study on optical care conducted by the Federal Trade Commission, Kwoka (1984) finds that the average quality of eye care is lower in regions with restrictions on advertising. Moreover, Liang and Ogur (1987) find in an additional field study that licensing rules that restrict the use of dental hygienists and assistants increased the average price of a dental visit by 11 percent in 1970 and 7 percent in 1982. They suggest that if these price increases do not produce any quality benefits, then consumers are worse off (Liang and Ogur 1987). There could be benefits of such regulations if exams by higher-quality dentists lead to the discovery of dental problems that, if left untreated, could result in teeth and gum deterioration, which could lead to a decline in overall health. Lacking in the licensing literature is the attribution of the total increase in the price of the service due to regulation and economic gains, where part of this increase could reflect an increase in quality or a greater demand for the service with a resulting increase in prices.

Another method of determining whether licensing has an impact on the quality of a service is through the premiums charged to individuals in regulated and unregulated states. The rationale for this evaluation is that if licensing serves to keep out incompetent potential practitioners relative to states that do not have licensing, then there would be a reduction in lawsuits for the service, which could lead to lower premiums. One of the main private and social functions of the insurance industry is to assess and monetize risk. A way to evaluate whether licensing has an influence on reducing risk is to examine if insurance premiums are reduced based on the licensing coverage in a state. In discussions with officials at a major national insurance company, their view was that licensing makes an occupation more visible and sets up rules and regulations that make lawsuits easier to file. The impact of this more structured procedure would drive up premiums. The greater visibility for the occupation and the greater ability to file lawsuits because of licensing's structure compensate for any potential benefits from the quality aspects of licensing from the perspective of the insurance industry. Overall, there is little evidence that licensing greatly improves the overall quality of services received when one also takes into account the number and quality of reduced services received by those at the lowest part of the income distribution.

Overall, the analysis of demand and quality does not show significant benefits of occupational regulation. There is little evidence that occupational regulation has a major effect on either the quality of service received by consumers or on the demand for the service other than through potential price effects. Another aspect of licensing that is often overlooked is its influence on innovation. Some have argued that board members of large corporations should be licensed (Freeman 2008). Although in some cases it may reduce problems related to ethical behavior or enhance skill sets, it could reduce innovation by prohibiting outstanding entrepreneurs. For example, Bill Gates and Steve Jobs did not finish college and would be ineligible to be on licensed boards of directors, but they nonetheless enhanced innovation and creativity in information technology through their technical and managerial skills and created some of the highest value-added innovations in the last 30 years.

THE NET EFFECTS OF OCCUPATIONAL LICENSING

There is no assurance that the services actually received by consumers are positively related with the quality of the inputs, and the distinction between the number of inputs employed and the quality of service outputs received may not be consistent. For example, a less competent dentist may require multiple attempts to fill a tooth to the same standard that a more skilled dentist could accomplish once. There is little to no published research on the relationship between performance on the licensing exam and an individual's ability to perform on the job. Even for occupations with lower general education requirements, such as cosmetology, job-specific training often is costly and sometimes longer than one year, with an apprenticeship followed by a state-licensing exam. These requirements may result in fewer practitioners, and lower-income and lower-educated practitioners may result in reduced access to the services provided. This can result in a distribution of resources from lower-income consumers, who now have to pay higher prices or have less access to a service such as haircuts or dental services. For example, an unlicensed restaurant server would have to pay more to a licensed dental hygienist or dentist for his dental health.

CONCLUSIONS

This chapter examines the curious issue of occupational licensing from a number of different perspectives and has five main findings. First, occupational licensing raises wages among those who have attained a license, but less so for those who are just covered by a licensing statute. In addition, the longer an occupation has been licensed, the greater the influence of the regulations on wage growth and employment changes. Second, occupational regulation reduces the interstate migration of several regulated occupations, such as public school teachers and lawyers. A consequence is a potential geographic misallocation of labor resources because this form of regulation reduces the ability of licensed workers to move across state lines to potential jobs. Third, the evidence suggests that occupational licensing raises the prices of regulated services. Fourth, these regulations may serve as a form of social insurance that may reduce the worst outcomes of certain types of risky services, such as medicine, yet provide some assurance by the government that the regulated services are of minimal quality. Unfortunately, the evidence thus far does not support the assertion that more heavily regulated services are of higher overall quality. In addition, the evidence about the influence of occupational licensing on average quality is murky at best. Whether occupational licensing enhances quality depends on the situation or task, and the profession that is being regulated.

Fifth and finally, the net effect of occupational licensing is that it enhances wages and benefits, raises prices, and reduces interstate migration; however, it has no measurable effect on the quality of the services provided to consumers. This is an issue that is presented from a perspective of licensing as a way to limit supply and restrict entry and thereby drive up wages. All these issues have contributed to the labor market institution of occupational licensing being a stealth form of regulation that has unusual and curious effects on the guild-ridden labor market, consumers, and the public.

Notes

1. A basic examination of the national costs of licensing could be developed as follows: suppose that the entire 15 percent wage premium for licensing mentioned above is from economic rents (as opposed to enhanced human capital), and further assume that labor supply is perfectly elastic and the labor demand elasticity is 0.5 and there are 38 million licensed workers (Hamermesh 1993). As a consequence, the impact would be in 2.8 million fewer jobs with an annual cost to consumers of $203 billion.
2. For additional examples see Carroll and Gaston (1981).
3. This value is lower than the 38 percent found by Kleiner and Krueger

(2013) in the survey conducted by Westat in 2008. This difference may reflect the larger sample size of the Harris data, which is almost four times the size of the Westat sample, the sample selection criteria, or the method of data collection (phone survey versus an online survey). In addition, there was no validity check on the quality of the responses by occupation in the Harris data. The number of state-level observations varies from 146 in Tennessee to 222 in the District of Columbia, and averages 193 per state.
4. See Kleiner (2006, Table 3.3) for a full listing of price effects of occupational licensing.

Chapter 4
Battles among Licensed Occupations

In the unionized part of the construction industry, there is sometimes a dispute over which craft is allocated a task on a job site. Unions and arbitrators decide which union will get to do the work of, say, building a wall. Should the occupation be the members of the bricklayers union, the laborers' union, or the carpenters' union? Similar to these jurisdictional disputes in the trade union sector in construction, occupational regulation has similar disputes in, for example, health care over who should provide well-child physical exams. Should it be the physician, physician's assistant, the nurse practitioner, or another specially trained health care provider? In other parts of construction work, should architects or interior designers provide the blueprints for the interior of a nursing home? When the work is very similar, should physical therapists or occupational therapists have the legal right to help, for example, disabled individuals within their homes?

HEALTH CARE

Understanding the consequences of contested terrains in regulated markets is particularly important in the health sector because it is especially subject to occupational regulation by the government. This sector is a particularly important economic factor. In 2009 the health sector accounted for about 18 percent of U.S. gross domestic product, and expenditures on provider services represented about 21 percent of total expenditures on health services (Centers for Medicare and Medicaid Services 2014). The health sector is also central in terms of employment; in 2012 it employed about 11.7 percent of all workers in the United States, and the share of workers in the health sector is expected to grow over the next 10 years (BLS 2014). At the same time, the core health occupations (e.g., physicians, nurses, and dentists) are universally licensed, and over three-fourths of nonphysician health workers also work in licensed occupations (Kleiner and Park 2010). If regulations have even small effects on wages and prices, then the aggregate cost of the regulations could be large in absolute dollars. The implications of proposed regulations are currently on the agenda in many states. The National Conference of State Legislatures reports that across the 54 state/territorial governments it monitors, 1,795 bills dealing with licensing tasks—or, as it is often called, scope of practice bills—were proposed during the two-year period from January 2011 to December 2012, and about 20 percent of these bills were adopted.

Studies of occupational licensing have shown the influence of licensing when regulations are introduced or become more stringent (Cathles, Harrington, and Krynski 2010; Cox and Foster 1990; Kleiner and Todd 2009). A key question relates to the issue of the influence of occupational regulations on wages, employment, and prices when regulations are changed in ways that alter the boundaries and shared work space between two occupations. For example, what are the effects of regulations that affect the scope of practice afforded to nurse practitioners?

Nurse practitioners are registered nurses who have obtained additional training through a master's or PhD degree program (Dueker et al. 2005; Harper and Johnson 1998). They are trained to diagnose and treat common illnesses and injuries, manage chronic illnesses, prescribe medications, and provide counseling. Nurse practitioners face a variety of state-specific occupational regulations that restrict their activities and their relationship with physicians. Three important regulations for nurse practitioners are those that involve limitations on prescription authority, the ability to practice independently, and the ability to be reimbursed by insurers for their services.

Policy Assessments of Nurse Practitioner Regulations

Based on the large number of states that are considering changing their statutes on occupational regulations (as noted earlier), there is evidence that state governments continue to be interested in altering their scope of practice regulations. For example, nurse practitioners who live on the border of Illinois and Missouri find that they are allowed to perform more tasks in Illinois than Missouri. One illustration is provided in the following comments: "As an advanced nurse practitioner with offices in Illinois and Missouri, I have a unique perspective. . . . Treatment for bronchitis can include cough syrup with codeine, and back pain may require a pain medication. In Illinois, after examination and diagnosis, I can write prescriptions (for drugs such as cough syrup with codeine). In Missouri, I need to delay the patient and interrupt the physician to have him prescribe the medications. This creates unnecessary delays and may require extra trips for the patient" (McQuaide 2007, p. C3).

Physicians have generally opposed broadening the scope of tasks that nurse practitioners are allowed to perform. For example, the Missouri State Medical Association was largely opposed to providing nurse practitioners with the ability to prescribe controlled substances. It supported alternatives in which nurse practitioners had only partial or short-term prescription rights: "The medical association wants limits on how much nurse practitioners could prescribe, capping the amount of medicine to enough for three to five days, for example, just to fill an immediate need before the patient could see a physician" (Lieb 2008 [online]).

These cases seem to represent the kinds of arguments made by nurse practitioners and physician organizations that lobby state governments. For economists or policy analysts, one concern is that these statements do not offer much information about the underlying market or social problems that scope of practice regulations is intended to address. Moreover, discussions about scope of practice regulations pay little attention to the possibility of unintended consequences. For instance, the public health implications seem to be an important missing piece of the discussion of prescription authority in Missouri. Under the "small doses framework" described by the Missouri State Medical Association, for example, it is possible that patients who visit a nurse practitioner for convenience reasons may forgo a second follow-up visit to a physician. In that case, the small dose restrictions could increase the chances that patients complete a partial dose of antibiotics, which could generate more antibiotic-resistant infections in the future. Besides the public health concern, the two-visit approach might substantially diminish any efficiency gains from granting more authority to nurse practitioners.

Physician advocacy groups often lobby state politicians to preserve laws requiring physician supervision for nurse practitioners. For example, in a recent review in the popular press, Elizabeth Dears, a senior vice president for the Medical Society of the state of New York, said in testimony to lawmakers that removing doctor oversight of nurse practitioners "would seriously endanger the patients for whom they care" (Pettypiece 2013, pp. 27–28). This perspective lends some support to the view that quality and safety concerns are the main justification for scope of practice laws considered at the state level. However, evidence that physician supervision of nurse practitioners improves patient safety is rarely offered.

What can we learn from these case studies? One issue is that physician lobby groups think that at least some consumers would like to substitute nurse practitioner visits for physician visits, and that concerns about service quality and patient safety are common arguments used to oppose expanded authority for nurse practitioners. In addition, relaxed state licensing provisions resulted in an increase in the wages of nurse practitioners and a reduction in the earnings of physicians, but they had no influence on deaths or malpractice premiums.

LICENSED AND CERTIFIED OCCUPATIONS IN CONSTRUCTION—ARCHITECTS VERSUS INTERIOR DESIGNERS

Occupations that are only certified and include tasks that overlap with those of licensed professionals are at a disadvantage in the labor market because the state statutes and administrative procedures declare what work must be completed only by licensed workers and not by certified ones; it is common for these statutes to disproportionately favor licensed professionals over certified ones. A specific job task in the construction industry that overlaps the work of interior designers and architects is developing blueprints of the interior design of commercial structures and verifying that these blueprints meet all state and local requirements. This approval process is called "signing and sealing the blueprints." Initially, only architects or interior designers working under the direct supervision of architects were allowed to provide this service. By 2012 all states allowed architects to implement sign and seal, but only 11 states allowed designers to do the task. Who is allowed to sign and seal, or offer final approval of blueprints, is a major issue for both interior designers and architects because it is lucrative and provides control over the final plans for the blueprints for building interiors of new construction.

For example, Georgia recently partially deregulated architectural services to allow interior designers to sign and seal. The bill amending the Georgia law that allows registered interior designers to draft, sign, and seal their own technical drawings for state approval was introduced in the legislature in 2009. Ryan Day, the associate director of Government and Public Affairs at ASID, when describing the need for this regulation, stated that "previous requirements called for architectural or structural review even though there were no structural alterations in the design plans. These requirements significantly inflated project costs and increased costs for consumers" (ASID 2005). The bill to amend the statute was met with opposition from the Georgia chapter of the American Institute of Architects (Georgia AIA), which prepared a 17-page document, "Vote No on SB 28 and HB 231," that outlined problems with the proposed bill. The issues are summarized in the following 2009 statement by Georgia AIA president Michael Lowry: "It is important that we contact our state legislators today and tell them that we do not support this bill because it represents an expansion into areas of 'Life Safety,' where interior designers do not have adequate training" (Lowry 2009 [online]). The "Vote No" document, however, did not provide any evidence that interior designers could not competently develop, sign, and seal the interior blueprints for commercial structures. Further, Georgia AIA president Lowry called for architects to "draft a letter to [their] senator urging them to oppose this bill" (Lowry and Perpall 2009). However, the Georgia AIA efforts were unsuccessful, and the bill became law in June 2010.

The consumers of architectural services and interior designers may be the immediate beneficiaries of the deregulation of architects. Following deregulation, consumers may be able to purchase the services of similar or perhaps even better quality from interior designers at a lower price.[1] The Georgia law now permits designers to work without architects' supervision, which may positively influence designers' incomes and employment. In contrast, the Georgia statute may have the opposite influence on architects' incomes and employment. Therefore, Kleiner and Vorotnikov (2012) focus on the effects of the introduction of sign and seal regulations and other such state statutes covering these two occupations on practitioners' wages and employment.

According to ASID (2010), the goal of interior designers today is to become regulated and eventually licensed by government. The rationale is that interior designers must become licensed in order to maintain legitimacy in their occupation relative to their complements and competitors in construction design, such as architects and engineers, in order to maintain their job tasks and income.

In the related engineering occupation, government regulation had evolved by the 1960s to include civil, electrical, mechanical, and industrial engineers. Since at that time only engineers could sign off on initial and final construction design and implementation of final construction, interior designers assumed an inferior position among occupations offering construction services. Moreover, architects were solely responsible for developing the initial structural design, which further diminished the role of interior designers. Over time, state and local governments have generally gained a more important role in determining the work process requirements in the construction industry. Government statutes or administrative procedures have gradually become the sole determinants of the appropriate types of labor inputs in construction. Within this institutional environment, interior designers figure that the only way for them to access certain types of work in such a growing field is to also become a licensed occupation; therefore, they have lobbied for licensing in a number of states and sought legal status for drafting construction blueprints.

Recent estimates from Kleiner and Vorotnikov (2012) suggest that giving interior designers the ability to provide the sign and seal service increases their earnings, and higher earnings are associated with more individuals entering the occupation. There are no such effects on the earnings or employment of architects. These findings suggest that architects and interior designers are more likely to be complements than substitutes in the production of sign and seal services. Architects could inappropriately allocate their resources when they try to interfere with the passing of sign and seal legislation.

LICENSED OCCUPATIONS THAT DO SIMILAR TASKS—PHYSICAL THERAPISTS AND OCCUPATIONAL THERAPISTS

The previous examples of occupations that are battling for mandates to do work legally show where architects have the upper hand in one of two ways: by being licensed for a much longer time or by being a licensed occupation dealing with one that was certified; namely, interior designers. In this case I examine the effects of occupational regulations on the practice restrictions faced by two overlapping occupations: physical therapists (PTs) and occupational therapists (OTs). These occupations are female dominated, they require graduate degrees to practice, and they have some overlap covering the same tasks. Across different situations, the services of a PT may function as either a substitute or a complement for the services of other medical professionals such as an OT. It is possible, for example, that PTs provide a set of services that are very similar to those offered by OTs but that are offered with a greater emphasis on factors such as convenience, personal attention, or specialization that are important to some patients in some situations. In short, PTs are an ideal example of an occupation with training and productive capacities that in some cases overlap with other occupations like OTs. This overlap means that the content and context of the work provided by PTs depend on a variety of occupational regulations that have varied across states and over time.

I look at these two occupations in order to understand in a more detailed way how occupational regulations affect labor market outcomes in the United States. Unlike other examinations of occupations that focus on ones that were dominant and subordinate, OTs and PTs are equivalent in terms of their incomes, prices charged, education, and tasks (Kleiner and Park 2010; Kleiner and Vorotnikov 2012; Kleiner et al. 2014). This examination shows how two occupations that have some overlap where regulations could matter for their labor market outcomes.

There is a large amount of empirical literature devoted to estimating the wage and employment effects of licensing regulations, and it includes work related to a variety of health occupations.[2] The literature concerned with overlapping occupations where substitution and complements may be important is much smaller and more recent. OTs and PTs are plausibly complementary because patients who visit an OT for basic health services also may be referred to a PT for more complex care. More generally, using an OT for low-complexity home care may free up time for PTs to specialize in more complex care—for example, muscular/skeletal development, which is essential to mobility and could be more lucrative. Some of these regulatory preferences may depend on the industrial organization of the medical sector. One conjecture is that health workers whose compensation depends in part on the economic performance of a particular health care firm might be less supportive of regulations that force the firm to adopt production processes that are not efficient. There is some empirical work on the regulation of other overlapping occupations. Kleiner and Park (2010) provide evidence that occupational regulations may alter the boundaries between the work tasks of dentists and dental hygienists, and may affect the earnings of both occupational groups. For example, Marier and Wing (2014) study regulations that define whether a hygienist may independently perform particular dental procedures: allowing hygienists to perform the service leads to lower prices for that service. Stange (2011) finds that increases in the supply of nurse practitioners and physician assistants at the county level do not directly increase utilization of health services, but they do lead to small gains in utilization in geographical areas that offer more independence to them, as measured by an index of regulations and by prescription drug authority. The examination of outcomes in labor markets that are closely connected to scope of practice regulations being studied allows us to trace the effects of the regulations across different occupations, such as PTs and OTs.

INSTITUTIONAL BACKGROUND

> The impact of different state licensure laws for the two professions in terms of the need for physician referral would certainly have workforce implications, whether this supports collaboration or points to growing differences between the two professions is still to be determined. In addition to concerns over the efforts to achieve unrestricted access directed by physical therapists, some occupational therapists are protesting what they believe to be added language in physical therapy practice acts in the area of "functional training in self-care and in home, community or work reintegration." Although this terminology has been in physical therapist education program accreditation criteria and practice acts for many years, the American Occupational Therapy Association has taken the position that this terminology is evidence of PTs encroachment into the scope of practice of OT. (Fisher and Keehn 2007, p. 26)

There is a distinctive difference in the general work of OTs and PTs. Occupational therapists train or retrain individuals to do general work that allows patients to work independently, whereas physical therapy focuses on physical rehabilitation and muscular and skeletal improvements. However, there are several areas where the two occupations overlap. These are areas of modality or method of treatment, wound care, and orthopedics and foot care. A key issue for both occupations is to get insurers to pay for direct access rather than being billed through a medical facility or a physician's office. Another key element for both occupations is how they bill through Medicare and how they are reimbursed for care.

Occupational Therapists

Occupational therapists define their work as follows:

> The therapeutic use of everyday life activities (occupations) with individuals or groups for the purpose of participation in roles and situations in home, school, workplace, community, and other settings. Occupational therapy services are provided for the purpose of promoting health and wellness and to those who have or are at risk for developing an illness, injury, disease, disorder, condition, impairment, disability, activity limitation, or participation restriction. Occupational therapy addresses the physical, cognitive, psychosocial, sensory, and other aspects of performance in a variety of contexts to support engagement in everyday life activities that affect health, well-being, and quality of life. (American Occupational Therapy Association 2014, p. 2)

According to the BLS (2014), the entry level requirement is a masters' degree. However, many in the occupation, including those at the occupational association, see the entry qualifications as a doctoral degree.

In contrast, PT tasks are noted as follows: "Physical therapists help people who have injuries or illnesses improve their movement and manage their pain. They are often an important part of rehabilitation and treatment of patients with chronic conditions or injuries" (BLS 2014).

The current entry point into the occupation as of 2016 is a doctoral degree, which is a professional degree that requires three years of classroom work and internships beyond a bachelor's degree. This is the requirement established by the major accrediting body for the occupation and is the default of most state licensing boards. Key elements for both these occupations are direct access to the patient and the billing of procedures for Medicare and health insurance.

Regulating Physical Therapists and Occupational Therapists

Physical therapy as an occupation gained much greater public attention as a medical intervention and use following World Wars I and II. During and following these conflicts, wounded soldiers used a combination of surgery and noninvasive procedures such as physical therapy. The number of PTs grew, and their procedures generally involved similar processes and standard patient care. The physical therapists then formed organizations that were the initial movers to obtain occupational licensing across states. Pennsylvania was the first state to license PTs in 1913, followed by New York in 1926. In 2003, Kansas became the last state to license the occupation.

In a similar manner, OTs were regulated much later than PTs. Florida was the first state to license OTs in 1975. In 2013, Colorado licensed occupational therapists, but Hawaii did not pass a law fully licensing occupational therapists until 2014. Occupational therapists were licensed decades after PTs, and only recently have most of the states chosen to fully regulate.

Empirical estimates show that occupational licensing raises the wages of both practitioners, and that the duration—how long the occupation has been licensed in the state—is the dominant influence on wage determination. Occupational licensing also is associated with a reduction in hours worked. The ability of PTs to have direct access to patients is associated with a reduction in hourly earnings for OTs, suggesting some substitution for certain services across the two occupations. The findings show that the introduction of a licensing statute reduces the relative number of both OTs and PTs. There is also a negative influence on hours worked as a consequence of licensing statutes. Also, for physical therapists, the duration of licensing is associated with a reduction in the relative number of practitioners. The ability of these two occupations to be both complements and substitutes for one another provides new evidence on how regulated occupations influence one another.

CONCLUSIONS

With the growth in the number of licensed occupations, it is not surprising that the tasks of regulated occupations may overlap. Since the tasks that are legal are determined by the legislature, governor, or administrative boards, political pressure may determine which occupations are allocated tasks. This is an especially important issue in health care, where dentists and dental hygienists may contest which tasks are appropriate for each occupation. Similarly, doctors and nurse practitioners may contest which occupation can perform routine and sophisticated tasks. In some occupations, where the occupations have similar levels of skill and training, such as PTs and OTs, the allocation of work is determined by the boards and the legislature. Even outside health care, occupations such as architects and interior designers battle for the right to provide sign and seal provisions for the designs of the interiors of buildings. For the occupations that are battling to provide services, the legislature and regulatory boards substitute their views of the appropriate occupation to provide the service rather than consumers.

Notes

1. The statement about the potential quality effects is based on the fact that only interior designers who acquire sufficient education and work experience and pass tests are allowed to develop and sign and seal their blueprints of interior design. Furthermore, although 11 states allow interior designers to sign and seal, and Louisiana introduced this regulation in 1985, we did not find any complaints filed against interior designers by customers who were unsatisfied with the service.
2. See Kleiner (2006) for a review of the empirical literature on wage-determination effects of licensing.

Chapter 5

Occupational Licensing in Different Institutional and International Contexts

Millions of Europeans, from bartenders to soccer stars, have to deal with what might be called the certification complex—a requirement that they be certified to pursue their jobs in a time-consuming process dating back to 19th-century apprenticeships. Economists say it is a big reason behind Europe's high unemployment and lagging productivity.

—John Miller, *Wall Street Journal*, August 16, 2004

As this newspaper article suggests, the regulation of occupations is perceived to be a major factor in the lack of efficiency in the labor market and a contributor to lagging productivity and unemployment in Europe. Is this the case, and do the European methods of regulating occupations have different labor market outcomes from those in the United States? Does occupational licensing influence the labor market the same way in the United States relative to other nations with different institutional and cultural settings? Are the wage effects of occupational licensing similar to that found in the United States? Would the same theories that apply to the U.S. legal and cultural setting also influence Europe and China? This chapter will attempt to answer how occupational licensing works in these settings. More specifically, the chapter focuses on many interesting legal conditions of occupational licensing in the European Union (EU), with illustrations and applications to the United Kingdom (UK) and China.

OCCUPATIONAL REGULATION IN THE EUROPEAN UNION

Observing licensing in Europe provides a comparison of this institution relative to its consequences in the United States. The focus of U.S. licensing is on control of entry and mobility across states, with little attention to the prices charged, method of payment, or barriers to advertising. In contrast, entry in the EU is somewhat easier and usually shorter for entry into the professions. For most occupations, joining occurs immediately after high school, though this process is highly competitive. Students matriculate into the professions and usually finish their professional education, which is subsidized in large part by the government, at an earlier age than in the United States. Following entry, there tend to be many more constraints on work, which include the location, prices charged, and the lack of an opportunity to provide information to consumers on the quality of the service through advertising. In the licensed health professions, the employer is often the government or is heavily subsidized by national funds. Unfortunately, there have been no analytical examinations of the impact that licensing in these nations has on the quality of service received in the EU. This stands in contrast to the relatively large number of studies that have examined licensing in the United States. For the most part, the empirical work shows that licensing has modest to no impact on quality relative to a regime of certification or registration.

If national inequality is low and constraints on the occupation are high, then price and wage impacts are likely to be modest. On the other hand, the impact of this regulatory policy where there are few financial incentives to succeed may lead to less effort because wage variations are small, or because the more able seek occupations where the financial constraints are less limited. In addition, innovation, creativity, and employment may be reduced in the regulated sector as relative financial incentives in the regulated sector are small, but entry requirements are tough.

For a number of occupations in Europe, prospective professionals must satisfy the requirements set by national governments and professional associations. This usually means passing a licensing exam and possibly meeting educational, residency, moral character, and fitness requirements. For example, physicians, nurses, and teachers are commonly required to be licensed to practice their professions throughout the EU. Perhaps less well known is that hundreds of other occupations are also subject to licensing regulations. Real estate and travel agents, manicurists, podiatrists, golf instructors, beekeepers, stonemasons, car mechanics, musical instrument manufacturers, corset makers, and potters are just some of the more than 800 professions that, according to the European Commission, are affected by occupational regulation in at least one European country (Koumenta et al. 2014).

No comprehensive information exists as to how many European workers are subject to occupational regulation. As was mentioned earlier in this book, occupational licensing in the United States directly affects about 29 percent of workers (Kleiner and Krueger 2013), which is substantially more than those affected by other labor market institutions, such as the minimum wage or unionization. Similarly, it is unknown whether the number of European workers affected by licensing is increasing or decreasing. However, for the United States, we know that this number has been systematically growing for the past 60 years. Thus, the first objective of this section is to show the prevalence of occupational regulation in the EU and provide a broad description of occupational regulation.

Table 5.1 shows the number of occupations that are licensed in each EU nation in 2012. The EU Single Market Regulated Professions Database (maintained by the EU Commission) includes information on whether various occupations are licensed in each country.[1] Drawing on this source, we know, for example, that lawyers, physicians, and nurses are licensed professions in all countries (i.e., there are some tasks that are reserved for these professions in each country). Architects and mechanical engineers also are often licensed, while real estate agents, financial brokers, and ski instructors are licensed

Table 5.1 Licensed Occupations in the EU-27, 2012

	Number of licensed professions
Estonia	14
Latvia	16
Lithuania	27
Sweden	38
Bulgaria	39
Luxembourg	48
Romania	48
Ireland	57
Cyprus	62
Finland	63
Hungary	75
Malta	75
Belgium	78
Portugal	85
Germany	86
Italy	86
Netherlands	87
Denmark	90
France	90
Greece	98
Slovak Republic	109
Spain	112
United Kingdom	131
Slovenia	135
Austria	151
Poland	162
Czech Republic	215
Total EU	2,277

SOURCE: The EU Single Market Regulated Professions Database (accessed in spring 2012) from Koumenta et al. (2014).

only in some countries. Unfortunately, there is no systematic source of data on professions subject to registration, certification, or accreditation. Consequently, the focus in the chapter is on licensing.

The data were collected to match information on licensed professions with labor force survey micro data sets from the European Labour Force Survey, a large household sample survey providing data on labor participation of employees and self-employed aged 15 and over, living in private households.[2] This method of data collection means we are collecting data on the coverage of workers rather than those who have attained a license. National statistical institutes in each member state are responsible for selecting the sample, preparing the questionnaires, conducting the direct interviews among households, and forwarding the results to Eurostat in accordance with the common coding scheme.[3] In our subsequent analysis, we pool the observations from the four successive quarters in 2012 to produce an annual data set.[4]

As Koumenta et al. (2014) point out, there are more than 800 occupations licensed in at least one country and over 2,700 occupation-country combinations. The Baltic states, Sweden, and Bulgaria have fewer than 40 licensed occupations, while the Czech Republic, Poland, Austria, and Slovenia have more than 130. Differences among countries are very large and reflect the diverse types of activities subject to licensing in different countries. They do not reflect the prevalence of licensing in the workforce, as the number of practitioners within different occupations may vary.

Because it is difficult to determine the exact proportion of workers affected by regulation in the mixed group (where some are licensed and others are not), it is difficult to estimate the proportion of workers subject to licensing. However, it is possible to estimate the maximum and the minimum number of workers subject to regulation.[5] Table 5.1 reports the number of licensed occupations by country based on these occupation codes.

Table 5.2 gives the estimated number of employed individuals in each of the 27 countries in the EU in 2012 that are influenced by

Table 5.2 Prevalence of Occupational Regulation in EU-27 Countries, 2012

Country	Prevalence of occupational regulation		
	Upper bound	Lower bound	Upper-lower
Estonia	0.03	0.03	0.00
Latvia[a]	0.06	0.03	0.03
Lithuania	0.07	0.06	0.01
Ireland	0.11	0.08	0.02
Romania	0.11	0.10	0.01
Malta	0.14	0.11	0.03
Sweden	0.14	0.11	0.04
Bulgaria[a]	0.15	0.04	0.11
Finland	0.15	0.10	0.05
Netherlands	0.16	0.10	0.06
Luxembourg	0.20	0.11	0.09
France	0.20	0.13	0.07
United Kingdom	0.21	0.11	0.10
Portugal[a]	0.21	0.07	0.14
Slovenia	0.22	0.11	0.11
Slovak Republic	0.23	0.12	0.10
Hungary	0.23	0.14	0.09
Spain[a]	0.26	0.08	0.17
Belgium	0.26	0.16	0.10
Greece[a]	0.26	0.08	0.18
Poland	0.27	0.14	0.12
Italy[a]	0.27	0.06	0.21
Austria	0.29	0.15	0.14
Cyprus[a]	0.30	0.09	0.21
Germany[a]	0.31	0.04	0.27
Czech Republic	0.39	0.17	0.22
Denmark[a]	0.43	0.13	0.30
Total EU	0.24	0.09	0.15

NOTE: Estimates are based on EULFS data for 2012.
[a] Countries for which only three-digit International Standard Classification of Occupations codes are available in the EULFS survey.
SOURCE: Koumenta et al. (2014).

occupational regulation relative to their unregulated counterparts. The results show considerable variation across countries that largely reflect the different data used to compile the estimates. The results from the table show that between 9 and 24 percent of European workers are subject to occupational licensing, which is between 19 and 51 million individuals. These are among the first estimates of the prevalence of occupational regulation coverage in the European Union to be produced. The percent licensed even at the higher bound is lower than the U.S. estimates in the high 20-plus percent range.

The countries in Table 5.2 are sorted from the lowest to the highest percentage of workers that are licensed. The Baltic states, Ireland, Romania, Malta, Sweden, Bulgaria, and Finland all have less than 15 percent of the labor force influenced by occupational licensing (Koumenta et al. 2014). This group also includes the Netherlands and France. The 9 countries with the highest prevalence of regulation include nations such as Spain, Italy, and Germany.

Having many occupations that are licensed does not mean that the percent of the workforce that is licensed is high. These results are not always in line with those obtained at the occupation level in Table 5.1. For example, there is a commonly held view that certain countries, such as Greece, Italy, and Cyprus, are overregulating their occupations, but these assertions are linked more to the number of individuals working within licensed occupations rather than to the actual proportion of occupations licensed. On the other hand, while Denmark licenses only 90 occupations (and is thus in the intermediate category in Table 5.1), such arrangements could cover a significant proportion of its workforce. Similarly, Cyprus licenses only 62 occupations, but up to 30 percent of the workforce is affected by these regulations.[6] Through the work by Mario Pagliero and others in the European Union and Britain to document the level of occupational licensing by nation in Europe, the data documented in these tables are informative; however, trends still have not been able to be developed on the direction of occupational regulation in the European Union (Koumenta et al. 2014).

As shown in Chapter 1, Poland is in the process of deregulating many of its national occupational labor markets (Kleiner and Lachowska 2014). The Poland Prime Minister's office (Prime Minister's Office [Poland] 2012) has stated that liberalizing access is expected to have the following three consequences:

1) Removing the barriers to enter regulated professions will result in higher employment. In fact, the prime minister's office has stated, "According to expert estimates, deregulation may increase employment within the [occupations] concerned by 15–20 percent" (Poland Prime Minister's Office 2012).

2) There will be lower prices and better quality services in the sectors that deregulate access to professions.

3) Administrative costs will be lower than the costs of maintaining the current regulatory system.

ANOTHER EXAMPLE: OCCUPATIONAL LICENSING IN THE UNITED KINGDOM

Although this chapter presents basic data on occupational regulation in the EU, it is particularly informative to examine a country that, in contrast to most of the other EU nations, has documented more thoroughly the growth of occupational regulation in recent years. The United Kingdom, given that the size and the relative openness of its labor market are closer in institutional structure to the United States than most of the other nations in the EU, is particularly interesting. In addition there has been more analysis of occupational licensing in the UK.

By comparison, the UK regulates more occupations than Germany and the Mediterranean economies, such as Italy, Greece, and Portugal. Somewhat surprisingly, with 131 regulated occupations, the UK has one of the highest proportions of regulated occupations in the EU. Differences among countries are very large and reflect the diverse types of activities subject to licensing in different countries. They do not reflect the prevalence of licensing in the workforce, as the number of practitioners within different occupations may vary. The prevalence of licensing in the UK is between 11 and 21 percent, which places it in the group of countries with intermediate regulation (16–26 percent).[7]

As a basis of comparison, two decades after the closed shop was outlawed in Britain, entry into a sizable and growing proportion of all jobs in Britain has been restricted through occupational licensing by government (Bryson et al. 2012; Metcalf and Stewart 1992). In a closed shop, union membership is a precondition for doing a job. A precondition under occupational licensing is possession of a government-issued license to practice in order to work. Similar to the United States, working for pay within the occupation in the UK without a government license is an offense punishable by fines and/or incarceration under the appropriate licensing statutes.

Recent attempts to estimate the wage effect of licensing in the UK follow the same approach as that in the United States. Drawing on the 2008 Labour Force Survey, a large survey of UK employees, Humphris, Kleiner, and Koumenta (2011) show that licensing is associated with a 13 percent wage premium once human capital and labor market characteristics are controlled for. The study provides one of the first overall wage impacts of licensing in the UK, and the estimates are quite similar to the influence of the closed shop on wage determination (Metcalf and Stewart 1992). Also, the impact of licensing on wages in the UK is similar to that in the United States.

Occupational licensing in the UK has been growing in a manner similar to the United States. By 2010, 14 percent of all jobs undertaken by UK employees were subject to licensing by the government, a growth of over two percentage points in just a decade, but still well below the U.S. estimates. Also like the United States, the wage premium in the UK is positively related to the stringency of the occupational licensing requirements. In addition, for the UK, the premium increases with the length of time since occupational licensing was first implemented. However, wage increases have not occurred for occupations that have become licensed within the last decade (Bryson et al. 2012). One reason for this finding may be that individuals are grandfathered in, and it takes them time to leave or retire from the occupation. Furthermore, it takes time for the licensing board to implement requirements (such as tests and continuing education) that may reduce the number of individuals that enter or stay in the occupation. A similar rationale has been applied to the gradual emergence of a union wage premium following plant-level unionization in the United States (Freeman and Kleiner 1990; Lee and Mas 2012).

INSTITUTIONAL DETAILS OF OCCUPATIONAL REGULATION IN THE UNITED KINGDOM

The UK approach to occupational regulation has many similarities with those found in other Commonwealth countries, such as Australia and Canada, but has some marked differences with the U.S. approach. It involves a variety of diverse institutional structures, including general and industry-specific law, as well as practices based on custom. For example, it can be statutory, meaning that the requirement for a license is set down in statute, or it can be voluntary. In the former case, it largely follows the approach so that professions are granted status by an Act of Parliament, indicating that regulation is at the national level. Also, the approach can vary depending on the range of products or services that are licensed—an individual with a specific job title can provide all products and services covered by that occupation (known as protection of title), or a specific job title can enable the individual to undertake certain activities or provide only specific services (known as protection of function).

This latter form of regulation does not restrict individuals from entering the profession, but it places restrictions on the activities they are allowed to perform as part of the profession. For example, an electrician can carry out electrical installations, but a licensed electrician has to inspect these installations and certify their safety. Also, regulation can vary depending on whether the license is issued by an occupational body or a government organization, or whether the license is issued on a local basis, usually by a local authority. Although there is national licensing, in certain cases local areas can have authority over the issuance of the license. Regulatory bodies in the UK are independent of any branch of government, but they work closely with government departments when reviewing occupational regulation issues.

The majority of occupations in the UK are licensed nationally; taxi drivers, who are issued a license at a local authority level, are an exception. Requirements for obtaining a license or becoming registered with a professional body can include passing an industry-specific exam, demonstrating work practices, and passing a medical or criminal record check. Finally, a license in the UK can either be permanent or have to be renewed periodically to demonstrate continued fitness to practice.

Based on these dimensions, occupational regulation in the UK can take the following forms: certification or registration. Certification, or accreditation, is the process in which a relevant authority assesses whether practitioners meet a minimum set of predetermined criteria that demonstrate competence and knowledge in a specific area. A private nonprofit industry body is usually responsible for overseeing the process and granting the certificate. As in the United States, certification is not mandatory; therefore, a noncertified practitioner also may provide similar services. However, given that certification indicates the achievement of a certain level of skill, consumers may be prepared to pay a premium for using a certified practitioner as opposed to a noncertified one.

Registration, on the other hand, may be voluntary or mandatory—the law requires practitioners to be registered (e.g., doctors), and it involves practitioners to meet certain standards before they can enter the register of qualified practitioners in the field. Requirements for registration may include attaining certain educational qualifications and passing exams. Registration with the relevant body may involve a statutory protection of a title, in that only those who are members of such a body may call themselves by that title (known as protection of title). For example, it is not a requirement to hold a license to describe oneself or to practice as a surveyor, but to use the title Chartered Surveyor, one must be a member of the Royal Institute of Chartered Surveyors. Using a protected title without being registered with the relevant regulatory body is an offense that carries a financial penalty. This has many similarities to certification in the United States.

NONTRADITIONAL LICENSING: CHINA

Similar to the UK and most of the EU, China has licensing that is primarily at the national level. Workers' efforts to become certified or licensed throughout China have greatly increased in recent years. Employees and college students have put considerable effort toward obtaining occupational certificates and licenses. For example, in 2003, 0.9 million people applied for the certified public accountant (CPA) licensing examination in China. In 2007 and 2010, this increased to 1.06 million and 1.3 million, respectively (*China Statistical Yearbook 2003–2010*). By 2012 the value had increased to 1.8 million who took the CPA licensing examination in China; this represents a 13.6 percent increase in the number of examinees from 2011.[8] The Ministry of Human Resource and Social Security (MHRSS) agency estimates that in 2007 alone about 10 million people obtained at least one occupational certificate.

Occupational certificates are becoming increasingly important in employment, wage, and promotion decisions. A survey of job seekers in China suggests that 52 percent of the respondents think that under the same conditions, job candidates with more certificates have an advantage in the labor market.[9] Some firms also reward employees for obtaining additional occupational certificates; given the same job, an employee's base salary will increase by $80–$160 per month for certain types of certificates.[10] However, despite the general growth in the number of certificates and the widespread opinion that occupational certificates can bring advantages with respect to employment and pay, there is evidence to indicate that certification can enhance wage determination in China (Chi, Kleiner, and Qian, forthcoming). The national occupational regulation system in China is different from the primarily state-by-state regulation in the United States.

As mentioned, occupational regulation in the United States takes three forms: registration, certification, and licensing. Registration is the least restrictive form of regulation and licensing the most restrictive, since monetary and incarceration penalties can be incurred for providing the service for pay without governmental approval (Kleiner 2000, 2006; Kleiner and Krueger 2013). Similarly, China has occupational certification and licensing regulations. As in the United States, certification in China is less restrictive than licensing. Certification permits any person to perform the relevant job, but the government administers an examination and certifies those who have achieved the level of skill for certification. Hiring uncertified individuals, however, carries no legal consequences. The certification system in China can be traced back to the 1950s. After economic reform, occupational certification became more widespread in the labor market and was increasingly accepted by both employees and employers as a credentialing mechanism.

In China, licensing is more restrictive than certification; under the licensing regulation, working in an occupation without a license is illegal. Penalties for practicing without a license include fines and imprisonment. For example, according to the Criminal Law of the People's Republic of China, Article 336, people practicing medicine without a license are deemed as "unlawfully practicing." They may be sentenced to 1–3 years' imprisonment, may be fined, or may be both imprisoned and fined. If such a practice causes severe harm to patients, punishment could increase to imprisonment of 3–10 years. Licensing requirements include educational or training prerequisites, examinations, internship, and residency in the profession. As an important labor market institution, the occupational licensing system in China was introduced after economic reform started in 1979. China's legislative system is known as a uniform legal hierarchy with multiple levels. Within the hierarchy, the order of the effect of laws begins with the constitution, down to national laws passed by the Standing Committee of the National People's Congress, administrative regulations, decisions, and decrees (promulgated by the State Council and ministries and commissions of the State Council), and finally, local regulations (Paler 2005). Local authorities (provinces) have limited legislative power. Relevant to occupation licensing, the regulations were formulated and promulgated by the state council and its ministries and departments. Thus, there is no variation across provinces in licensing regulations. The uniformity of licensing regulations across China is an important distinction from the United States, where there is substantial variation across and even within states. Unlike licensing rules, for some professions, certification rules were made by provincial authorities, often in conjunction with professional associations, where there is an opportunity for the associations to limit entry or raise requirements for maintaining a license.

Among the many types of occupational certificates, the majority are those issued by the MHRSS. As of 2012, 1,055 jobs out of the total of 1,838 jobs catalogued in China's Occupation Classification System are covered by the MHRSS certification system.[11] These 1,055 jobs are from 87 generic production and service occupations. There are five levels of certificates for manual labors (including entry level, intermediate, and advanced skilled labor, and technician I and II) and three levels for service workers (i.e., entry level, intermediate, and advanced). Examples of MHRSS certificates include those for blue-collar workers, such as welder, turner, and fitter, as well as those for professional workers, such as human resource manager, logistic manager, psychiatrist/psychological consultant, nutritionist, and IT manager. Professional associations or leading companies in the IT profession, such as Cisco Certified Network Associate (CCNA) and

Microsoft Certified Solutions Master (MCSM) for IT professionals, also provide certificates.

Of the 1,055 MHRSS-certified jobs, 90 are licensed.[12] For these jobs, workers must obtain a license to work; without it, workers cannot be employed or practice on their own. The employer who hires an unlicensed worker for these jobs will be given a warning and fined up to $160 per case. In addition to the 90 jobs, there are 31 other licensed professional occupations, including lawyer, medical doctor, nurse, pharmacist, accountant, real estate appraiser, architect, construction engineer, and urban planner. These occupations are regulated by other government agencies and separate laws.

The influence of occupational licensing on wage determination in China is consistent with that found in the United States and the UK. Empirical analysis for China finds that licensing is associated with an average of 15 percent higher wages and certification with 13–14 percent higher wages based on survey data collected for China (Chi, Kleiner, and Qian, forthcoming). The findings are that the total fraction of certified or licensed workers in China is similar to that in the United States, but the licensing rate is likely significantly lower. This outcome may be related to the historical development of certification and licensing systems in China: the certification system dated to the 1950s and preceded the licensing system; it was more prevalent than the licensing system, and licensing (for physicians, lawyers, and architects) was developed only in recent years. Physicians began to be licensed in 1998; licensing for lawyers started in 1996, and architect licensing in 1995. More recently, nurses have been licensed since 2008. Given these factors, it is not surprising that certification and licensing have similar influences on wage determination in China, given the historical evolution of these two institutions in that country.

SUMMARY AND CONCLUSIONS

Occupational licensing is a labor market institution that is important not only in the United States but in many other countries around the world. This chapter has documented this and evaluated its impact in the EU, the UK, and China. The level of occupational licensing is lower in the EU than in the United States, but the range of licensing in each country in the EU is wide, with an overall estimate of 14–24 percent. For one nation in the EU, the UK, there appears to be some growth in occupational licensing that is similar to that in the United States. Also, the influence on wage determination in the EU and China is not very different from the estimates on the wage determination in the United States, which is about 13 percent. In China the certification of occupations evolved much earlier than occupational licensing and has been rapidly growing in recent years. Nevertheless, the influence of licensing has been close to 14 percent, which is not far from the upper-bound estimate of 15–18 percent that has been found in the United States. The curious institution of occupational licensing is prevalent and has an important role in labor markets across many different nations and institutional contexts.

Notes

1. See http://ec.europa.eu/internal_market/qualifications/regprof/index.cfm?action=homepage (accessed May 28, 2015).
2. Persons carrying out obligatory military or community service are not included in the target group of the survey, as is also the case for persons in institutions/collective households.
3. For more details see http://epp.eurostat.ec.europa.eu/portal/page/portal/microdata/lfs (accessed May 29, 2015).
4. We focus on 2012, as it is the most recent available year in the EU Labour Force Survey data set. Some changes in regulation have occurred since then, but we cannot yet match them with labor force data. Earlier changes in the regulatory status of professions in European countries are not recorded in the EU Single Market Regulated Professions Database.

5. The upper bound is computed by summing the proportion of workers in the regulated and mixed groups and assumes that all workers within the International Standard Classification of Occupations (ISCO) codes are subject to regulation, while the lower bound is the proportion of workers in the regulated group and assumes that none of the workers within the remaining ISCO codes are regulated. The true prevalence of occupational regulation may lie anywhere in this interval.
6. The correlation between upper and lower bound is high (0.53) but different from 1. This is partly due to the variability across countries in the precision of occupational classifications in the European Labour Force Survey. Some countries (Latvia, Bulgaria, Portugal, Spain, Greece, Italy, Cyprus, Germany, and Denmark) report relatively coarse occupational codes in the European Labour Force Survey (three-digit level only). This implies that the interval between the upper and lower bounds is much larger. Lower bounds, for these countries, are particularly small, owing to the difficulty in classifying workers as definitely subject to occupational licensing (Koumenta et al. 2014).
7. The UK results are consistent with those reported by Bryson et al. (2012), allowing for some measurement error in both their and our calculations.
8. "The Number of Individuals Taking the CPA Examination Exceeds 1.8 Million in 2012" (in Chinese), China Accounting Net, February 17, 2012. http://www.canet.com.cn/zhongji/zjdt/201202/17-237023.html (accessed April 2013).
9. The estimate of 10 million people who attained occupation certificates in 2007 and the information about the survey of people's attitudes toward obtaining occupational certificates are both sourced from a newspaper article in the China Youth Daily: "Lost in Certification: Crazy for Certification Exams" (in Chinese), College Information Net, May 4, 2008. http://campus.chsi.com.cn/xy/news/dt/200805/20080504/6258116.html (accessed April 2013).
10. "Eight Certificates Obtained in Four Years of College: Blindness in Certification Exams," February 2, 2011 (in Chinese), n.p. XinHua Net. http://www.xinhua08.com/life/jd/201102/t20110222_314951.html (accessed April 2013).
11. Ministry of Human Resource and Social Security's Skill Certification Center (in Chinese), May 2011. http://www.cettic.gov.cn/zyjnjd/zyjnbz/2011-05/03/content_408249.htm (accessed April 2, 2013).
12. Decree of the Ministry of Human Resources and Social Security, No. 6, 2000, effective since July 1, 2000 (in Chinese). http://www.molss.gov.cn/gb/ywzn/2006-02/14/content_106425.htm (accessed April 2013).

Chapter 6

Policy Implications of the Evolution of Occupational Licensing in the United States and Elsewhere

> *The impossibility of any individual or small group conceiving of all the possibilities, let alone evaluating their merits, is the great argument against central governmental planning and against arrangements such as professional monopolies that limit the possibilities of experimentation. On the other side, the great argument for the market is its tolerance of diversity; its ability to utilize a wide range of special knowledge and capacity. It renders special groups impotent to prevent experimentation and permits the customers and not the producers to decide what will serve the customers best.*
> —Milton Friedman (1962, p. 160)

> *All professions are conspiracies against the laity.*
> —George Bernard Shaw (1906)

> *The modern state owes and attempts to perform a duty to protect the public from those who seek for one purpose or another to obtain money. When one does so through the practice of a calling, the state may have an interest in shielding the public against the untrustworthy, the incompetent, or the irresponsible.*
> —Robert H. Jackson in *Thomas v. Collins* (1945)

This book explains how licensing is varied and expanding in the U.S. labor market and is pervasive around the world. Yet, the comments above by Milton Friedman, George Bernard Shaw, and Robert Jackson state different views of the conceptual benefits and costs of occupational regulation. Within this context, what are potential policy implications of this growing labor market institution? This chapter identifies several potential changes that may be helpful in improving the functioning of the labor market. More specifically, what policies should be developed to decide who can perform which functions under the law? Certain policies can provide barriers to service provisions and drive up costs. As an example, there are restrictions on what tasks can legally be undertaken by dental hygienists relative to dentists and nurse practitioners relative to physicians. Second, occupational licensing is implemented by state boards, which can restrict geographic mobility and imposes labor market frictions. Third, by imposing time and monetary costs on the entry into certain occupations, licensing restricts job creation and impedes entrepreneurial activity. This can reduce innovation and creativity among a class of individuals as the Friedman comment above alludes to regarding innovation. For example, for electricians, an innovation such as plastic wiring may require a different safety protocol than copper wiring, but the licensing authority may require the older procedures. The delays in official protocol and implementation may lead, for example, to workplace injuries for electricians (Kleiner 2013).

This chapter will propose several policy reforms that attempt to deal with the problems that occupational licensing creates in the labor market. The first is the creation of federal guidelines, based on state economic and labor market conditions for occupational licensing boards. These guidelines will be established based on the demonstrated costs and benefits associated with licensing in various occupations or tasks. Second, the policy recommendations will suggest greater reciprocity across state boundaries in the recognition of occupational licenses, and third, they will examine the use of certification of occupations as an alternative for many current and emerging occupations.

Because occupational licensing varies by state, another channel through which licensing can affect employment is by reducing mobility. The patchwork of regulations raises the cost of cross-state mobility for workers in these occupations. This will result in slower adjustment costs to regional economic shocks, which can result in higher unemployment. Licensing also can lead to higher prices for services because it restricts employment (Bond et al. 1980; Cox and Foster

1990; Kleiner and Kudrle 2000; Kleiner and Todd 2009; Shepard 1978).

While it is not possible to precisely estimate the effects of substantially reducing licensing, both the logic of the issue and the available evidence suggest that such a reduction could translate into significantly higher employment, better job matches, and improved customer satisfaction. Low-income consumers, in particular, would benefit because reduced barriers to entry would lower the prices of services provided, for example, from plumbers and electricians (Cox and Foster 1990; Shapiro 1986). Without doing a detailed analysis at the occupation-by-occupation and state level, it would be impossible to say which occupations can be justified based on quality consideration, though when studies have been conducted they have found at least in some cases that licensing reduces employment and increases prices but does not result in better services. For example, Kleiner and Kudrle (2000) find that occupational licensing of dentists does not lead to improved measured dental outcomes but is associated with higher prices of certain services, likely because there are fewer dentists.[1] Similarly, Kleiner and Todd (2009) find that tougher licensing of mortgage brokers is not associated with fewer housing foreclosures but is related to higher-priced mortgages.

The existing body of work completed on occupational licensing offers just a sample of the possible reforms that could be done. For example, a sensible reform that has been identified is to allow dental hygienists to operate a practice without the supervision of a dentist. However, taking a piecemeal approach, I propose five general reforms that states and localities could take that would rationalize future and existing regulations:

1) Prospective evaluations. State and local governments should require benefit-cost analysis prior to the new occupational licensing requirements. The burden should be on the government together with the interest groups representing the occupation to demonstrate that the social benefits of

these requirements exceed the economic costs. If the benefits to the public exceed the costs, governments and the interest groups should also demonstrate that the proposed regulations are the least restrictive means of furthering the goals of the regulations.[2]

2) Retrospective evaluations. State and local governments should develop and execute a plan to evaluate existing occupational licensing requirements. The evaluations could be based on existing studies or new analyses. When the costs of the evaluations are shown to exceed the benefits, the requirements should be modified or dropped.

3) Reciprocity. When licensing is deemed to be in the interest of the public, weighed against the economic costs, states and localities should accept, as much as possible, licenses granted in other states.

Proposal 3 would facilitate cross-state mobility and make it more difficult for special interests to tighten regulations in order to increase their monopoly power over the supply of labor in a given state. Under this proposal, targeting the 10 states with the most mobility between them would go a long way toward solving the problem.[3]

If state and local governments were to seriously undertake proposals 1–3, the available evidence suggests that employment in these occupations would grow and monopoly rents would fall. The main fiscal cost on states would be from the loss of fees for occupational licenses.

There is a way for governments to raise revenues while at the same time curtailing the use of occupational licensing and increasing employment:

4) Impose a surcharge or tax on workers in licensed occupations where there is evidence that the licensing leads to barriers to entry perhaps as much as the rents within the occupation.

Proposal 4 is more unorthodox, but it is based on sound economic principles. When occupational licensing leads to entry barriers, workers in those occupations enjoy monopoly rents. This surcharge would draw from those rents without adverse employment consequences. Moreover, as has been well documented, when there are employment restrictions, even if they can be justified based on their benefit to the public, special interest groups have incentives to tighten the restrictions beyond what is optimal. Taxing rents would reduce the incentive for these groups to engage in this kind of lobbying.

5) Certification policies as a substitute for licensing.

Proposal 5 is based on the analysis of the benefits and costs of licensing; there may be some occupations where lesser forms of regulation, such as certification or registration, or even no regulation, may be beneficial. For example, locksmiths, ballroom dance instructors, shampooers, interior designers, upholsters, pet groomers, and hair braiders may not pose sufficient risk to health and safety to warrant the full regulation or "right to practice" of licensure. An additional policy would be to suggest that occupations such as these be moved by the state from licensing to certification or other lesser forms of regulation or no regulation.

THE FEDERAL ROLE

Although there are occupational licensing requirements at the federal level, it is state and local rules that by far have the broadest reach. Research also has found that licensing has the most pronounced effects when it is subject to multiple layers of jurisdiction. Local requirements tend to have less bite. For these reasons, the federal government is well suited to promote a set of best practices, such as those listed above. This could be achieved through a combination of moral suasion and monetary incentives.

Under this plan, states would be encouraged to submit a proposal that outlines specific steps they aim to take to reduce unnecessary licenses or allows licensed practitioners to more easily move between states, counties, or cities. The proposals should describe steps they plan to take to reduce barriers to entry in specific occupations (e.g., dental hygienists and nurse practitioners), as well as broader "process" reforms they would undertake, such as 1–3 above. The plans would be reviewed by a panel of experts in the area that could include academics, business and labor leaders, and government officials, and a partial award would be distributed to the most meritorious plans, with the remaining amount withheld until certain benchmarks have been met.

Because these practices do not impose a substantial fiscal burden on states, the incentives do not have to be large for this to have an effect on state take-up. The incentives from the successful "Race to the Top" fund were $4.3 billion, which is far smaller than even conservative estimates of the costs of licensing. The monetary incentives are scalable, but importantly on a dollar for dollar basis, their economic benefits are likely to exceed costs. As a start, the Obama administration submitted a budget that included a $15 million dollar appropriation to implement such a program (Porter 2015).

Calls to reduce occupational licensing barriers to interstate mobility have come from the executive branch of the U.S. federal government, including the U.S. Department of the Treasury and the U.S. Department of Defense (2012). These policy recommendations have been made in part because the families of military personnel have had a difficult time moving across states and pursuing their careers because of the variations in state licensing laws. The Department of Defense views this effect as a hardship on military families. At a minimum, the ability to recognize other state licenses, similar to recognizing driver's licenses across states, would serve to help military families as well as assist the economy in general in greatly reducing structural or frictional unemployment due to state regulation barriers. It would also allow licensed workers to maximize their incomes and productivity by enabling them to move across state lines without institutional constraints. In fact, in many cases it is harder to move across states for occupations such as dentists and optometrists because potential professionals have to take or retake examinations. Licensing has also been cited as being a barrier for upward income mobility for individuals with low incomes or wealth. For example, occupational licensing was recently cited in Representative Paul Ryan's (R-WI) national approach to reduce poverty in his 2014 monograph, *Expanding Opportunity in America* (Ryan 2014, p. 66). He noted the following:

> Another category of rules and regulations that can hurt low-income families are state and local occupational-licensing regimes. These requirements often prevent workers from entering or advancing in the workforce. Government at all levels requires licenses to perform certain occupations. In some cases, such as medical doctors, this requirement is appropriate. However, in other cases, these licensing requirements merely protect entrenched incumbents.
>
> Eliminating irrational or unnecessary licensing requirements would not be a panacea, but it would open up new opportunities for low-income families and reduce costs for consumers. The vast majority of these licensing requirements are the result of state and local laws. State and local governments should begin to dismantle these barriers to upward mobility.

In concert with other federal programs that he identifies in his monograph, Rep. Ryan sees reducing occupational regulation for low-income individuals as an important antipoverty program. Specifically, he sees reducing government barriers to entry into a job through occupational licensing as an element in reducing poverty in the United States (Ryan 2014).

The federal government reimbursement or grant funding requirements also enhance the growth of occupational licensing. For example, the federal government will deal with or fund only licensed surveyors for contracts or grants involving surveying roads or parks. As a result, the states think they have the need to license surveyors. In health care, occupational therapists, in order to be reimbursed under

Medicare or other federal programs such as the Affordable Care Act, must have a state license. In these cases, the federal government puts pressure on the states to license additional occupations or ramp up the requirements to attain a license.

AT THE STATE LEVEL

Although occupational licensing has been growing, several proposals have been made to slow its growth in favor of certification. For example, in Minnesota the legislature passed a bill out of the Minnesota Senate Commerce and Consumer Protection Committee that explicitly favors certification over licensing in both 2011 and 2012. The bill states that

> no government shall require an occupational license, certification, registration, or other occupational regulation that imposes a substantial burden on the person unless the government demonstrates that it has a compelling interest in protecting against present and recognizable harm to the public health and safety, and the regulation is the least restrictive means to furthering that compelling government interest. . . . [A]n individual who brings an action or asserts a defense under this section has the initial burden of proof that the statute or administrative rule or a government practice related to the statute or rule substantially burdens the individual's right to engage in an occupation not prohibited by law. If the individual meets the burden of proof . . . the government must then demonstrate by clear and convincing evidence that the government has a compelling interest in protecting against present and recognizable harm to the public health and safety, and the regulation is the least restrictive means for furthering that compelling governmental interest.[4]

This is an illustration of "model legislation" on occupational licensing that is currently being proposed by the Institute for Justice, a libertarian public interest law firm that has handled numerous cases for individuals who have challenged occupational licensing laws on the grounds that they limit free speech or the freedom to work.

The proposed Minnesota statute goes a long way toward favoring a policy of the least possible regulation of occupations by the government, and it allows the courts to determine whether an individual has been economically harmed or if there are compelling health and safety issues that warrant the occupation to be licensed. Consequently, the burden of proof shifts from the individual to the state, which must show that there is a potential health and safety hazard from an individual not being licensed in order to perform their job tasks. One possible drawback of the proposed licensing regulation in Minnesota is the increased litigation costs if individuals who thought that they could do the work were engaged in a significant number of lawsuits. The legal costs could be balanced by the reduction in economic rents to the members of the licensed occupations and increased aggregate output for the services of the members of the licensed occupations.

Other states have also moved toward deregulating occupations but use somewhat different approaches. For example, as was mentioned in Chapter 1, in April 2014, the governor of Indiana signed legislation called the Senate Enrolled Act 421, which required the Indiana Professional Licensing Agency to study and establish a commission on the concept of self-certification registration as an alternative to licensing and issue a report to the legislative council before October 1, 2014. According to the governor, the report must include the following:

- occupations that may be included on the list
- whether to provide title protection for the individuals included on the list (a form of certification)
- enforcement provisions that would be used
- a description of auditing and maintenance of the list
- the cost of establishing and maintaining a list
- the cost of an individual applying for and renewing inclusion on the list

A potential result of the commission is the conversion of most of Indiana's licenses to voluntary private certifications for a wide variety of occupations, most of which are non-health-related ones. In addition, it would allow citizens to add their names and private certification numbers to a state-run registry. The changes aim to move the regulatory process toward private sector accreditation rather than public boards, which are often dominated by the members of the occupation. However, the private sector monitors also may be subject to pressures to limit entry by the occupations they serve. For example, credit agencies failed to monitor financial institutions during the financial crisis of 2008 because they were intimidated by the larger banks and afraid that they might lose their business. An additional issue is that states sometimes abrogate their oversight duties by allowing the professional associations to set standards that are often beyond what is needed for health and safety. For example, in many states, the educational licensing standards for physical therapists come from the professional association's boilerplate policy and may not consider what is best for the patient or for competent care, prices, and access to the services. Consequently, the professional associations establish the de facto terms of entry and reciprocity rather than the state licensing boards.

INTERNATIONAL POLICY ISSUES

Occupational regulation is an important labor market institution in the EU, and it is growing in China. It is becoming a dominant labor market institution in the EU, covering up to one-quarter of the labor force, although the vast majority of occupations in China are certified rather than licensed (Chi, Kleiner, and Qian, forthcoming). It deserves more attention than it currently has been receiving by researchers and policymakers. The EU Commission has focused its policy on reducing barriers to mobility and fostering labor movement within the EU (Koumenta et al. 2014). Although some of the research has not found any major influence of the legal restrictions on migration, EU policymakers should not ignore the fact that becoming licensed involves a cost to the individual, not the least in relation to the skill and location-specific investments it entails. While steps toward reciprocity can partly address the former, the latter still remains a key consideration in an individual's cost-benefit analysis to migrate. In addition, the length of time that occupational licensing has been in effect and the stringency of the entry requirements are both better predictors of a wage premium than whether the occupation is licensed in the EU. The wage effects of occupational licensing in the UK are similar to those found in the United States when human capital factors are taken into account, suggesting that there are economic returns to licensing in the UK.

Similarly, occupational regulation in China is rapidly increasing. The national occupational regulation system in China is different from the U.S. system of primarily state-by-state regulation. Similarly, China has occupational certification and licensing regulations. Using imputation based on occupation code and licensing rules, 9 percent of respondents would be licensed in 2003 (Chi, Kleiner, and Qian, forthcoming). This is much lower than the U.S. rate of about 29 percent in 2006. However, the wage effects are remarkably similar, showing the influence of occupational licensing to be about 14 percent. Again, the influence of licensing seems to be a fairly robust phenomenon across different nations and institutional settings.

SUMMARY AND IMPLICATIONS FOR U.S. OCCUPATIONAL LICENSING POLICY

This book provides a detailed, nontechnical overview of occupational licensing in the United States, China, the United Kingdom, and the European Union for students of the labor market, consumers, the public, and policymakers. Occupational licensing is an institution that rarely is discussed or receives the media attention that its size and scope warrant. It makes up about 29 percent of the U.S. workforce, up to 24 percent of the workforce in the EU, about 14 percent in the UK, and about 9 percent in China. The book examines the institution of occupational licensing from a historical perspective and offers a rationale for its existence and costs, an international perspective, and policy implications.

A major argument for licensing occupations is that it eliminates or reduces the consumer's risk of seeking the services from practitioners of an occupation. If testing and background checks "eliminate charlatans, incompetents or frauds" (Council of State Governments 1952), then consumers may be willing to pay a higher price for the services offered by the regulated occupation. A review of the body of theory from experimental economics and psychology shows that consumers value the reduction in downside risk more than they value the benefits of a positive outcome. This consumer preference for reducing the risk of a highly negative outcome has been called "loss aversion," which is an element of the prospect theory developed by Kahneman and Tversky (1979). For example, social welfare may be increased substantially by minimizing the likelihood of a poor outcome as a consequence of going to an incompetent physician, because the incompetent physicians have been weeded out as a result of licensing. Consequently, occupational licensing may also reduce patients' perceived benefits of receiving nonstandard but potentially highly effective treatment from an unlicensed practitioner of nontraditional medicine. Using the power of the state to both limit the downside risk of poor quality care and reduce the possibility of an upside benefit may be a trade-off that maximizes consumer utility or welfare. Evidence of the acceptance of this trade-off can be found in the growth of occupational licensing during the past century in many countries (Kleiner 2006).

The gains from an unregulated service can be potential benefits from greater free market competition of lower prices and greater innovation without the constraints of a regulatory body, such as a licensing board. The upside potential gain can be achieved through both the use of nonstandard methods or new research that has not been approved by the licensing agency as appropriate for the medical service (Rottenberg 1980). Deviations from prescribed methods of providing a service are discouraged by licensing boards and may even be found to be illegal. For example, not having a dentist on-site is illegal in the United States when providing a service such as teeth cleaning in some states. Dental hygienists generally are not allowed to "practice" without a dentist on-site, with the "site" being defined by statute or the dental board. In addition, dental hygienists generally are not allowed to open offices to compete with dentists in most states. Although this policy reduces the chance that a dental hygienist will fail to find a major disease that may require immediate attention, it also reduces the ability of the hygienist to provide the limited services that particular patients say they want. Moreover, there is little leeway for the dental service industry to provide new or innovative services without the risk of being found in violation of the licensing laws. The licensing laws give rise to the labor relations concept of "featherbedding," whereby in this case, dentists are required to be on the premises but do little observable productive work.

Consequently, for medical services, regulation through licensing can be the equivalent of a closed shop in unionized markets. Theoretically, higher wages are likely to result from restricted labor supply. Because closed shops in unionized markets are illegal in both the United States as a result of the Taft-Hartley amendments to the National Labor Relations Act and in the UK, it is interesting that, with respect to organized labor markets, a similar restriction to closed shops is nevertheless permitted in licensed medical occupations.

Certification grants title (occupational right-to-title) protection to persons meeting predetermined standards. It is often thought of as a better policy alternative than occupational licensing for three reasons:

1) Certification has benefits over licensing for workers. It does not fence out workers or cause the type of problems in labor markets that licensing does. Licensing may cause workers to lose the opportunity for upward mobility because of the bar-

riers to entry. A reduction in licensing requirements could enhance employment growth prospects in the state. Licensing further reduces the ability of workers to move across state lines and engage in work that is the most beneficial to them and to society. Certification of practitioners, when properly managed, does not have these negative features.

2) It is better for consumers. Similar to licensing, certification sends a signal to consumers about who has met the government's requirements. However, it does not reduce competition and gives consumers more choices for the kinds of services they want.

3) Certification can reduce the unnecessary and often excessive lobbying by occupational associations to try to convince legislators to enact licensing regimes under the assumption of protecting the public.

Moving to a system of certification rather than occupational licensing gives consumers more choices and provides useful information about the purveyor of the service. Many consumers and politicians say licensing protects against "loss aversion" and may be worth the costs of granting monopoly power to an occupation. In other words, consumers respond more to knowledge about bad services than good conditions, which suggests that they respond more to information that reduces their utility than to information that increases it; this is consistent with prospect theory (Kahneman and Tversky 1979). To illustrate, for an uninformed consumer who is considering brain surgery, licensing provides the guarantee that the provider of a service has at least finished medical school and taken a licensing exam. Nevertheless, a doctor who specializes in pediatrics and has never performed major surgery could legally perform brain surgery under most state licensing laws. Under certification, anyone who is not a certified brain surgeon could not argue that she has completed the course and passed the appropriate exams and claim to be a brain surgeon. If she claimed to be certified and was not, she would face legal penalties determined by the state. She could, however, legally perform the operation with the patient's consent. Under a regime of certification, the patient could have the surgery completed by a certified brain surgeon, a pediatrician, or a medical technician who has access to the latest technology on brain surgery. Information on all alternatives would be available to the consumer of the service, but insurance companies could put constraints on consumer decisions based on their knowledge of the procedure and legal liability issues.

Lists and reviews of practitioners similar to those maintained by the Better Business Bureau or Angie's List, a consumer-based service review website, provide some protection, but they have little enforcement powers beyond moral suasion. A central monitoring authority like the state, which screens potential applicants and provides greater assurance about the abilities of the individual, would be more useful, especially for low-income individuals or those with mental or physical disabilities. Without this enforceable "title protection," little quality assurance could be provided to the public on this listing of practitioners. The cost of being removed from the list of registered practitioners without the legal penalties of having "inappropriate skills" or competence may lead to insufficient consumer knowledge of the quality of the skill.

Without the legal costs of title infringement, service providers would have little economic incentive to be honest. Furthermore, it may not provide sufficient protection for providers of the occupation to undertake the investments that are required to advance in the field. If low-quality practitioners can claim to have the skills and expertise to perform a task, then optimal investments in human capital acquisition may not take place. Unlike lesser forms of regulation, certification allows consumers to select only those who have met the certification requirements established by the profession or any other services, and it allows for the purchase of lower-quality service but without the brand. This market alternative under certification can serve as discipline for the professions to not greatly limit barriers to entry. In conclusion, the central policy question for occupational licensing is, to what extent should the government protect the consumer and their families against their own bad decisions?

Notes

1. For additional examples see Carroll and Gaston (1981).
2. This proposal was recently introduced in the Minnesota State Legislature (2012).
3. Between 1995 and 2000, the 10 state pairs with the largest gross mobility between them were (New York, Florida), (New York, New Jersey), (California, Nevada), (California, Texas), (California, Arizona), (Florida, Georgia), (California, Washington), (California, Oregon), (California, Colorado), and (New Jersey, Pennsylvania).
4. For a detailed explanation of the statute, see Minnesota H.F. No. 2002, as introduced in the 87th Legislative Session (2011–2012), posted on the state website February 1, 2012 (Minnesota State Legislature 2012).

References

Akerlof, George A. 1970. "The Market for 'Lemons': Quality Uncertainty and the Market Mechanism." *Quarterly Journal of Economics* 84(3): 488–500.

Alexander, Adrienne, Chris Henjum, Jeremy Jones, Meg Luger-Nikolai, Aaron Rosenberger, and Caro Smith. 2009. *Regulating Interior Designers, Overview and Analysis of Public Policy*. Minneapolis, MN: University of Minnesota.

American Occupational Therapy Association. 2014. "Scope of Practice—Definition of Occupational Therapy." Bethesda, MD: American Occupational Therapy Association. https://www.aota.org/-/media/Corporate/Files/AboutAOTA/OfficialDocs/Position/Scope-of-Practice-edited-2014.PDF (accessed July 9, 2015).

American Society of Interior Designers (ASID). 2005. *The History of ASID: 30 Years of Advancing the Interior Design Profession*. Washington, DC: American Society of Interior Designers. http://asidcanv.org/students/student-legislative-resources (accessed July 9, 2015).

———. 2010. "Georgia Governor Signs Legislation to Recognize Registered Interior Designers." Press release. Washington, DC: American Society of Interior Designers.

Angrist, Joshua D., and Jonathan Guryan. 2003. "Does Teacher Testing Raise Teacher Quality? Evidence from State Certification Requirements." NBER Working Paper No. 9545. Cambridge, MA: National Bureau of Economic Research.

Apgar, William, Amal Bendimerad, and Ren S. Essene. 2007. *Mortgage Market Channels and Fair Lending: An Analysis of HDMA Data*. Cambridge, MA: Joint Center for Housing Studies, Harvard University.

Associated Press. 2013. "Pence Vetos License Bills for Dieticians, Others." http://www.ibj.com/pence-vetoes-license-bills-for-dietitians-others/PARAMS/article/41250 (accessed July 10, 2015).

Baker, Samuel. 1984. "Physician Licensure Laws in the United States, 1865–1915." *Journal of the History of Medicine and Allied Sciences* 10(2): 173–197.

Beck, Andrew. 2004. "The Flexner Report and the Standardization of American Medical Education." *Journal of the American Medical Association* 29(17): 2139–2140.

Benson, Johann, Jonathan Dworin, Thomas Garry, Jason Hicks, Teresa M. Schicker, and Anders Victor. 2014. "Diagnosing Healthcare in America: Impacts of Immigrants and Occupational Licensing." Professional paper. Minneapolis, MN: University of Minnesota, Humphrey School of Public Affairs.

Bond, Ronald, John E. Kwoka Jr., John J. Phelan, and Ira Taylor Whitten. 1980. *Effects of Restrictions on Advertising and Commercial Practice in the Professions: The Case of Optometry.* Staff report. Washington, DC: Bureau of Economics, Federal Trade Commission.

Branstad, Terry. 2013. "Licensure Legislation Vetoed by Governor Branstad." Ankeny, IA: Iowa Board of Certification. http://www.iowabc.org/PDFs/Letter_from_IBC_President.pdf (accessed July 14, 2015).

Bryson, Alex, John Forth, Amy Humphris, Morris M. Kleiner, and Maria Koumenta. 2012. "The Incidence and Labor Market Outcomes of Occupational Regulation in the UK." Paper presented at the Allied Social Science Associations annual meeting, held in Chicago, January 5–8.

Bureau of Labor Statistics. 2012. *Occupational Employment Statistics.* Washington, DC: U.S. Department of Labor, Bureau of Labor Statistics. http://www.bls.gov/oes/ (accessed December 12, 2012).

———. 2014. *Occupational Outlook Handbook,* 2014–15 ed. Washington, DC: U.S. Department of Labor, Bureau of Labor Statistics. http://www.bls.gov/ooh/healthcare/physical-therapists.htm (accessed October 17, 2014).

Carpenter, Dick M. II, Lisa Knepper, Angela C. Erickson, and John K. Ross. 2012. *License to Work: A National Study of Burdens from Occupational Licensing.* Arlington, VA: Institute for Justice.

Carroll, Sidney L., and Robert Gaston. 1981. "Occupational Restrictions and the Quality of Service Received: Some Evidence." *Southern Economic Journal* 47(4): 959–976.

Cartter, Allan M. 1959. *Theory of Wages and Employment.* Homewood, IL: R.D. Irwin.

Cathles, Alison, David E. Harrington, and Kathy Krynski. 2010. "The Gender Gap in Funeral Directors: Burying Women with Ready-to-Embalm Laws?" *British Journal of Industrial Relations* 48(4): 688–705.

Centers for Medicare and Medicaid Services. 2014. "National Health Expenditures Fact Sheet." Washington, DC: Centers for Medicare and Medicaid Services. https://www.cms.gov/Research-Statistics-Data-and-Systems/Statistics-Trends-and-Reports/NationalHealthExpendData/NHE-Fact-Sheet.html (accessed September 15, 2015).

Chi, Wei, Morris M. Kleiner, and Xiaoye Qian. Forthcoming. "Do Occupational Regulations Increase Earnings? Evidence from China." *Industrial Relations.*

China Statistical Yearbook. 2003–2010. Beijing: China Statistics Press, National Bureau of Statistics in China.

Council of State Governments. 1952. *Occupational Licensing Legislation in the States.* Chicago: Council of State Governments.

Cox, Carolyn, and Susan Foster. 1990. *The Costs and Benefits of Occupa-*

tional Regulation. Washington, DC: Bureau of Economics, Federal Trade Commission.

Cutler, David, and Ernst Berndt. 2001. "Introduction." In *Medical Care Output and Productivity*, David Cutler and Ernst Berndt, eds. Chicago: University of Chicago Press, pp. 1–11.

Dent v. West Virginia 129 U.S. 114 (1889).

Dranias, Nick. 2007. *The Land of 10,000 Lakes Drowns Entrepreneurs in Regulations*. Arlington, VA: Institute for Justice.

Dueker, Michael J., Ada K. Jacox, David E. Kalist, and Stephen J. Spurr. 2005. "The Practice Boundaries of Advanced Practice Nurses: An Economic and Legal Analysis." *Journal of Regulatory Economics* 27(3): 309–330.

Edlin, Aaron, and Rebecca Haw. 2014. "Cartels by Another Name: Should Licensed Occupations Face Antitrust Scrutiny?" *University of Pennsylvania Law Review* 162: 1093–1164.

Federman, Maya N., David E. Harrington, and Kathy J. Krynski. 2006. "The Impact of State Licensing Regulations on Low-Skilled Immigrants: The Case of Vietnamese Manicurists." *American Economic Review* 96(2): 237–241.

Feldman, Roger, and James W. Begun. 1978. "The Effects of Advertising: Lessons from Optometry." *Journal of Human Resources* 13(Supplement): 247–262.

Fisher, Gail, and Mary Keehn. 2007. "Workforce Needs and Issues in Occupational and Physical Therapy." Chicago: University of Illinois at Chicago. http://www.westga.edu/~distance/ojdla/spring161/workforce.pdf (accessed May 29, 2015).

Fitzgerald, F. Scott. 2008. *The Curious Case of Benjamin Button and Other Jazz Age Stories*. New York: Penguin Books. (Previously published as *Jazz Age Stories*. 1922. New York: Charles Scribner's Sons.)

Fixler, Dennis, and Mitchell Ginsburg. 2001. "Health Care Output and Prices in the Producer Price Index." In *Medical Care Output and Productivity*, David Cutler and Ernst Berndt, eds. Chicago: University of Chicago Press, pp. 221–270.

Flexner, Abraham. 1910. *Medical Education in the United States and Canada: A Report to the Carnegie Foundation for the Advancement of Teaching*. Bulletin No. 4. New York: Carnegie Foundation for the Advancement of Teaching, p. 346.

Ford, Ina Kay, and Daniel H. Ginsburg. 2001. "Medical Care in the Consumer Price Index." In *Medical Care Output and Productivity*, David M. Cutler and Ernst R. Berndt, eds. Chicago, University of Chicago Press, pp. 203–219.

Freeman, Richard B. 2008. *America Works: Critical Thoughts on the Exceptional U.S. Labor Market*. New York: Russell Sage Foundation.

Freeman, Richard B., and Morris M. Kleiner. 1990. "The Impact of New Unionization on Wages and Working Conditions." *Journal of Labor Economics* 8(1): S8–S25.

Freeman, Richard B., and James L. Medoff. 1984. *What Do Unions Do?* New York: Basic Books.

Friedman, Lawrence. 1965. "Freedom of Contract and Occupational Licensing, 1890–1910: A Legal and Social Study." *California Law Review* 53(1): 487–534.

Friedman, Milton. 1962. *Capitalism and Freedom.* Chicago: University of Chicago Press.

Friedman, Milton, and Rose Friedman. 1980. *Free to Choose: A Personal Statement.* Boston: Houghton Mifflin.

———. 1998. *Two Lucky People: Memoirs.* Chicago: University of Chicago Press.

Friedman, Milton, and Simon Kuznets. 1945. *Income from Independent Professional Practice.* Cambridge, MA: National Bureau of Economic Research.

Gittleman, Maury, Mark A. Klee, and Morris M. Kleiner. 2015. "Analyzing the Labor Market Outcomes of Occupational Licensing." NBER Working Paper No. 20961. Cambridge, MA: National Bureau of Economic Research.

Gittleman, Maury, and Morris M. Kleiner. Forthcoming. "Wage Effects of Unionization and Occupational Licensing Coverage in the United States." *Industrial and Labor Relations Review.*

Greene, Karen. 1969. "Occupational Licensing and the Supply of Nonprofessional Manpower." Washington, DC: U.S. Department of Labor.

Gross, Stanley. 1984. *Of Foxes and Hen Houses: Licensing and the Health Professions.* Westport, CT: Quorum Books.

Ham, Hwikwon, and Morris M. Kleiner. 2007. "Do Industrial Relations Institutions Influence Foreign Direct Investment? Evidence from OECD Nations." *Industrial Relations* 46(2): 305–328.

Hamermesh, Daniel S. 1993. *Labor Demand.* Princeton, NJ: Princeton University Press.

Han, Suyoun, and Morris M. Kleiner. 2015. "Analyzing the Duration of Occupational Licensing on the Labor Market." Paper presented at the Labor and Employment Relations Association Meetings, held in Pittsburgh, PA, May 30.

Harper, Doreen C., and Jean Johnson. 1998. "The New Generation of Nurse Practitioners: Is More Enough?" *Health Affairs* 17(5): 158–164.

Holen, Arlene. 1965. "Effects of Professional Licensing Arrangements on Interstate Labor Mobility and Resource Allocation." *Journal of Political Economy* 73(5): 492–498.

———. 1978. *The Economics of Dental Licensing.* Arlington, VA: Public Research Institute of the Center for Naval Analysis.

Humphris, Amy. 2013. "Conversations on Occupational Licensing." PhD thesis. London School of Economics.

Humphris, Amy, Morris M. Kleiner, and Maria Koumenta. 2011. "How Does Government Regulate Occupations in the United Kingdom and the United States? Issues and Policy Implications." In *Employment in the Lean Years: Policy and Prospects for the Next Decade*, David Marsden, ed. New York: Oxford University Press, pp. 87–101.

Jacobides, Michael G. 2005. "Industry Change through Vertical Disintegration: How and Why Markets Emerged in Mortgage Banking." *Academy of Management Journal* 48(3): 465–498.

Johnson, Janna, and Morris M. Kleiner. 2015. "Does Occupational Licensing Reduce Interstate Migration?" Paper presented at the W.E. Upjohn Institute for Employment Research, July 30.

Kahneman, Daniel, Jack L. Knetsch, and Richard H. Thaler. 1991. "The Endowment Effect, Loss Aversion, and Status Quo Bias." *Journal of Economic Perspectives* 5(1): 193–206.

Kahneman, Daniel, and Amos Tversky. 1979. "Prospect Theory: An Analysis of Decision under Risk." *Econometrica* 47(2): 263–292.

Kaplan, Greg, and Samuel Schulhofer-Wohl. 2012. "Understanding the Long-Run Decline in Interstate Migration." Working paper. Minneapolis, MN: Federal Reserve Bank of Minneapolis.

Kapp, Diana. 2014. "When Uber Is the Family Chauffeur." *Wall Street Journal*, December 18, D:1–D:2.

Kleiner, Morris. 2000. "Occupational Licensing." *Journal of Economic Perspectives* 14(4): 189–202.

———. 2006. *Licensing Occupations: Ensuring Quality or Restricting Competition?* Kalamazoo, MI: W.E. Upjohn Institute for Employment Research.

———. 2013. *Stages of Occupational Regulation: Analysis of Case Studies.* Kalamazoo, MI: W.E. Upjohn Institute for Employment Research.

———. 2015. *Reforming Occupational Licensing Policies.* Washington, DC: Brookings Institution.

Kleiner, Morris M., Robert S. Gay, and Karen Greene. 1982. "Barriers to Labor Migration: The Case of Occupational Licensing." *Industrial Relations* 21(3): 383–391.

Kleiner, Morris M., and Alan B. Krueger. 2010. "The Prevalence and Effects of Occupational Licensing." *British Journal of Industrial Relations* 48(4): 676–687.

———. 2013. "Analyzing the Extent and Influence of Occupational Licensing on the Labor Market." *Journal of Labor Economics* 31(2): S173–S202.

Kleiner, Morris M., Alan B. Krueger, and Alex Mas. 2011. "A Proposal to Encourage States to Rationalize Occupational Licensing Practices." Princeton, NJ: Princeton University.

Kleiner, Morris M., and Robert T. Kudrle. 2000. "Does Regulation Affect Economic Outcomes? The Case of Dentistry." *Journal of Law and Economics* 43(2): 547–582.

Kleiner, Morris, and Marta Lachowska. 2014. "The Deregulation of Professions in Poland." Proposal submitted to the European Union Commission, February.

Kleiner, Morris, Allison Marier, Kyoung Won Park, and Coady Wing. 2014. "Relaxing Occupational Licensing Requirements: Analyzing Wages and Prices for a Medical Service." NBER Working Paper No. 9906. Cambridge, MA: National Bureau of Economic Research.

Kleiner, Morris M., and Kyoung Won Park. 2010. "Battles among Licensed Occupations: Analyzing Government Regulations on Labor Market Outcomes for Dentists and Hygienists." NBER Working Paper No. 16560. Cambridge, MA: National Bureau of Economic Research.

Kleiner, Morris M., and Daniel L. Petree. 1988. "Unionism and Licensing of Public School Teachers: Impact on Wages and Educational Output." In *When Public Sector Workers Unionize*, Richard B. Freeman and Casey Ichniowski, eds. Chicago: University of Chicago Press, pp. 305–322.

Kleiner, Morris M., and Richard M. Todd. 2009. "Mortgage Broker Regulations That Matter: Analyzing Earnings, Employment, and Outcomes for Consumers." In *Studies of Labor Market Intermediation*, David Autor, ed. Chicago: University of Chicago Press, pp. 183–231.

Kleiner, Morris M., and Evgeny S. Vorotnikov. 2012. "Complementarities and Substitutions between a Licensed and a Certified Occupation: An Analysis of Architects and Interior Designers." Presented at the Society for the Advancement of Socio-Economics annual conference, held in Cambridge, MA, June 28–30.

———. 2015. "The Economic Effects of Occupational Licensing among the States." Working paper. Minneapolis, MN: University of Minnesota.

Kleiner, Morris M., and David Weil. 2012. "Evaluating the Effectiveness of National Labor Relations Act Remedies: Analysis and Comparison with Other Workplace Penalty Policies." In *Research Handbook on the Economics of Labor and Employment Law*, Cynthia L. Estlund and Michael L. Wachter, eds. Cheltenham, UK: Elgar, pp. 209–247.

Koumenta, Maria, Amy Humphris, Morris Kleiner, and Mario Pagliero. 2014. *Occupational Regulation in the EU and UK: Prevalence and Labour Market Impact*. Final report. London: Queen Mary University of London.

Kwoka, John E. Jr. 1984. "Advertising and the Price and Quality of Optometric Services." *American Economic Review* 74(1): 211–216.

Langford, Carol. 2009. "Barbarians at the Bar: Regulation of the Legal Profession through the Admissions Process." *Hofstra Law Review* Winter: 1193–1224.
Lee, David S., and Alexandre Mas. 2012. "Long-Run Impacts of Unions on Firms: New Evidence from Financial Markets, 1961–1999." *Quarterly Journal of Economics* 127(1): 333–378.
Liang, J. Nellie, and Jonathan D. Ogur. 1987. *Restrictions on Dental Auxiliaries*. Washington, DC: Federal Trade Commission.
Lieb, David A. 2008. "Senate Bill Would Allow Nurses to Write More Prescriptions." *Missourian*, July 22. http://www.columbiamissourian.com/news/local/senate-bill-would-allow-nurses-to-write-more-prescriptions/article_6920730a-7ac0-5cae-9a3d-51b1c5102e7b.html (accessed July 23, 2015).
Liptak, Adam. 2014. "Regulatory Case in North Carolina Appears to Trouble Supreme Court." *New York Times*, October 14, A:24.
Lowry, Michael. 2009. "AIA Georgia Legislative Announcement HB 231 on the Floor Wed., 2/11/09." http://www.aiaga.affiniscape.com/associations/7807/files/Your%20email%20Legislative%20Alert%20-%20HB231%20has%20been%20sent.htm (accessed April 22, 2012).
Lowry, Michael, and Fred Perpall. 2009. "A Letter from Michael Lowry, AIA and Fred Perpall, AIA." http://www.aiaga.affiniscape.com/displaycommon.cfm?an=1&subarticlenbr=231 (accessed April 22, 2012).
Marier, Allison, and Coady Wing. 2014. "Effects of Occupational Regulations on the Cost of Dental Services: Evidence from Dental Insurance Claims." *Journal of Health Economics* 34: 131–143.
Maurizi, Alex R. 1980. "The Impact of Regulation of Quality: The Case of California Contractors." In *Occupational Licensure and Regulation*, Simon Rottenberg, ed. Washington DC: American Enterprise Institute for Public Policy Research, pp. 399–413.
McQuaide, Terry. 2007. "Expert Diagnosis: Should Nurses Be Able to Prescribe Controlled Drugs in Missouri?" *St. Louis Post-Dispatch*, October 31.
Metcalf, David, and Mark Stewart. 1992. "Closed Shops and Relative Pay: Institutional Arrangements or High Density?" *Bulletin* 54: 503–516.
Miller, John W. 2004. "Europe's 'Oudated' Job Rules: Some Say Certification Requirements Hinder EU Productivity." *Wall Street Journal*, August 16, A:11.
Minnesota State Legislature. 2012. HF 2002, as Introduced. St. Paul, MN: Minnesota State Legislature. https://www.revisor.mn.gov/bills/text.php?number=HF2002&session=ls87&version=list&session_number=0&session_year=2012 (accessed July 22, 2013).
Molloy, Raven, Christopher L. Smith, and Abigail Wozniak. 2011. "Inter-

nal Migration in the United States." *Journal of Economic Perspectives* 25(3): 173–196.

Moretti, Enrico. 2012. *The New Geography of Jobs*. New York: Mariner Books.

North Carolina State Board of Dental Examiners v. Federal Trade Commission (2014).

Ogilvie, Sheilagh. 2014. "The Economics of Guilds." *Journal of Economic Perspectives* 28(4): 169–192.

Pahl, Cynthia J. 2007. *A Compilation of State Mortgage Broker Laws and Regulations, 1996–2006*. Community Affairs Report No. 2007-2. Minneapolis, MN: Federal Reserve Bank of Minneapolis. http://www.minneapolisfed.org/publications_papers/pub_display.cfm?id=4983 (accessed May 1, 2013).

Paler, Laura. 2005. "China's Legislation Law and the Making of a More Orderly and Representative Legislative System." *China Quarterly* 182: 301–318.

Pashigian, Peter B. 1979. "Occupational Licensing and the Interstate Mobility of Professionals." *Journal of Law and Economics* 22(1): 1–25.

———. 1980. "Has Occupational Licensing Reduced Geographical Mobility and Raised Earnings?" In *Occupational Licensing and Regulation*, Simon Rottenberg, ed. Washington, DC: American Enterprise Institute, pp. 299–333.

Paul, Charles. 1982. "Physician Licensure Legislation and the Quality of Medical Care." *Atlantic Economic Journal* 12(4): 18–30.

Pettypiece, Shannon. 2013. "Anything You Can Do, I Can Do Better." *Bloomberg Business Week*, March 11–17, pp. 27–28.

Phelan, J. 1974. "Regulation of the Television Repair Industry in Louisiana and California: A Case Study." Washington DC: Bureau of Economics of the Federal Trade Commission.

Porter, Eduardo. 2015. "Job Licenses in Spotlight as Uber Rises." *New York Times*, January 27, B:1.

Prime Minister's Office (Poland). 2012. "Deregulation Concerning Access to Certain Professions." March 3. Warsaw, Poland: Prime Minister's Office.

Raphael, Steven. 2014. *The New Scarlet Letter? Negotiating the U.S. Labor Market with a Criminal Record*. Kalamazoo, MI: W.E. Upjohn Institute for Employment Research.

Reynolds, Jeff. 2015. "Idaho Governor Otter Vetoes New Regulations on Sign-Language Interpreters." *Heartland News*, April 24. http://news.heartland.org/newspaper-article/2015/04/24/idaho-gov-otter-vetoes-new-regulations-sign-language-interpreters (accessed July 10, 2015).

Rose, Nancy L., ed. 2014. *Economic Regulation and Its Reform: What Have We Learned?* Cambridge, MA: National Bureau of Economic Research.

Rottenberg, Simon. 1980. "Introduction." In *Occupational Licensure and Regulation*, Simon Rottenberg, ed. Washington, DC: American Enterprise Institute, pp. 1–10.

Ryan, Paul, 2014. *Expanding Opportunity in America: A Discussion Draft from the House Budget Committee*, Washington, DC, Committee on the Budget, U.S. House of Representatives.

Santayana, George. 1905. *The Life of Reason: Introduction and Reason in Common Sense*. Vol. 7, Book 1. New York: Charles Scribner's Sons.

Shaw, George Bernard. 1906. *The Doctor's Dilemma*. Royal Court Theater, Liverpool.

Schmidt, James A. Jr. 2012. "New and Larger Costs of Monopoly and Tariffs." Economic Policy Paper 12-5. Minneapolis, MN: Federal Reserve Bank of Minneapolis.

Shapiro, Carl. 1986. "Investment, Moral Hazard and Occupational Licensing." *Review of Economic Studies* 53(5): 843–862.

Shepard, Lawrence. 1978. "Licensing Restrictions and the Cost of Dental Care." *Journal of Law and Economics* 21(1): 187–201.

Stange, Kevin. 2011. "Occupational Licensing and the Growth of Nurse Practitioners and Physician Assistants: Effects on Prices, Quantity, and Access." Working paper. Ann Arbor, MI: University of Michigan.

Tenn, Steven Aaron. 2001. "Three Essays on the Relationship between Migration and Occupational Licensing." Unpublished dissertation. Department of Economics, University of Chicago.

Thomas v. Collins, 323 U.S. 516, 545 (1945).

Triplett, Jack E. 2001. "What's Different about Health? Human Repair and Car Repair in National Accounts and in National Health Accounts." In *Medical Care Output and Productivity*, David M. Cutler and Ernst R. Berndt, eds. Chicago: University of Chicago Press, pp. 15–96.

U.S. Department of the Treasury and U.S. Department of Defense. 2012. *Supporting Our Military Families: Best Practices for Streamlining Occupational Licensing across State Lines*. Washington, DC: U.S. Department of the Treasury and U.S. Department of Defense.

U.S. Executive Office of the President. 2013. "The Fast Track to Civilian Employment: Streamlining Credentialing and Licensing for Service Members, Veterans, and Their Spouses." Washington, DC: The White House, p. 27.

———. 2015. "Occupational Licensing: A Framework for Policymakers." Washington, DC: The White House, p. 76.

Wheelan, Charles J. 1998. "Politics or Public Interest? An Empirical Examination of Occupational Licensing." Unpublished dissertation, University of Chicago.

Author

Morris M. Kleiner is a professor at the Humphrey School of Public Affairs, and he teaches at the Center for Human Resources and Labor Studies, both at the University of Minnesota–Twin Cities. He has received many university teaching awards for classes in public affairs, business, and economics. He is a research associate in labor studies with the National Bureau of Economic Research in Cambridge, Massachusetts, and he serves as a visiting scholar in the economic research department at the Federal Reserve Bank of Minneapolis. He has been a professor at the University of Kansas, an associate in employment policy with the Brookings Institution, a visiting scholar in the Harvard University economics department, a visiting researcher in the Industrial Relations Section at Princeton University, a visiting scholar at the W.E. Upjohn Institute for Employment Research, and a research fellow at the London School of Economics. He received a doctorate in economics from the University of Illinois. He began his research on occupational licensing at the U.S. Department of Labor in 1976, while working for the Brookings Institution. His work has been supported by the National Science Foundation, the Department of Labor, the Department of Health and Human Services, the United Kingdom Commission for Employment and Skills, the Smith Richardson Foundation, the Kauffman Foundation, and the W.E. Upjohn Institute for Employment Research. In the United States, Professor Kleiner has provided advice on occupational regulation policy to the Federal Trade Commission, the Council of Economic Advisers, the Department of the Treasury, the Department of Justice, the Board of Governors of the Federal Reserve System, federal interagency statistical panels, state legislatures, and occupational licensing associations. Internationally, he has provided testimony on occupational regulation to United Kingdom cabinet officers and their parliamentary committees, to cabinet officials responsible for occupational regulation in Australia, and to officials of the European Union.

Index

The italic letters *f, n,* or *t* following a page number indicate a figure, note, or table on that page. Double letters mean more than one such item appear on a single page.

Accreditation. *See* Certificates
Advertising, quality information in, 41, 62
Affordable Care Act, 86
Agricultural occupations, beekeepers, 63
AIA. *See* American Institute of Architects
AIID. *See* American Institute of Interior Designers
Alabama, 22, 25, 29*f*
AMA. *See* American Medical Association
American Institute of Architects (AIA), 21
  as deregulation opponent in Georgia, 51–52
American Institute of Interior Designers (AIID), creation of, 20, 21
American Medical Association (AMA), 11
  control of medical workers, 15, 16
  state associations within, 49–50
American Occupational Therapy Association, 55
American Society of Interior Designers (ASID), 21
  pursuit of licensure laws by, 6, 20, 21–22, 24*n*6, 51, 52
Antipoverty programs. *See* Poverty reduction
Architects
  as licensed occupation, 51–52, 53, 63, 75
  overlapping tasks of, 20, 23, 47, 51, 52, 58
Arizona, 29*f,* 94*n*3
ASID. *See* American Society of Interior Designers
Australia, occupational licensing in, 70
Austria, 2012 data on numbers of licenses in, 64*t,* 65, 66*t,* 76*n*4

Baltic states. *See* Estonia; Latvia; Lithuania
Bonding, 23
  surety bonds in, 19–20, 24*nn*4–5
Branstad, Gov. Terry, vetoes of, 5
Breyer, Justice Stephen, on decision making, 37
Brokers. *See under* Financial industry; Mortgage industry
Bulgaria
  2012 data on numbers of licenses in, 64*t,* 65, 66*t,* 76*n*4
  licensed individuals in, 66*t,* 67
  upper and lower bound ISCO worker codes for, 64*t,* 65, 77*nn*5–6
Businesses as enterprises, 12, 80
  decision making and certificates in, 72–73

Cadillac effect, quality and cost in, 5, 17
California, 29*f,* 40–41, 94*n*3
Canada, occupational licensing in, 29*f,* 70
Capitalism and Freedom (Friedman), 16–17
Certificates, 75
  favored in reform legislation, 86–87, 94*n*4
  as government standard, 1, 61, 65, 71, 72
  intent of, as step toward licenses, 21, 62
  as less onerous regulation than licenses, 3, 73, 80, 83, 88
  licenses *vs.,* 55, 71, 91–93
  requirements for, 28*f,* 72
China, occupational licensing in, 72–75
  certificates in, 72–73, 77*nn*8–9
  legal hierarchy in, 74
  licensing in, 73–74, 75, 89–90
  MHRSS, 72, 74–75, 77*nn*11–12
  perspective of, 2, 6, 7

Cisco (firm), legal certificates issued by, 74
Closed shop, 69, 91
Collective bargaining, NLRA and, 13
Colorado, 9, 94*n*3
  workforce licensed in, 29*f*, 57
Competition, 27, 62
  among occupations in same industry, 50–53
  restriction of, 10, 12, 20, 22
Construction occupations
  contractors, 39
  electricians, 3, 14, 70–71, 80
  engineers, 14, 20, 21, 23, 52, 63, 70–71, 75
  laborers, 47, 74
  plumbers, 3, 14
  welders, 74
  See also Architects; Interior designers
Consumer prices
  certified *vs.* licensed services and, 55, 71, 90
  deregulation effect on, 6, 23, 68, 85
  licensing effect on, 7, 26, 35–38, 44, 45*n*4, 80
Consumers, 40, 81
  licensing costs to, 4, 5, 23, 25, 32, 44*n*1
  as politically unorganized, 4–5
  prevention of public harm to, 6, 12, 36, 58, 79, 90
Cost-benefit analysis, 89
  government interventions and, 25, 26, 79
  policy reform and, 81–82, 83, 94*n*2
Council on Medical Education, AMA, 16
Craft occupations
  blacksmiths, 12
  body artists, 25
  bricklayers, 47
  carpenters, 47
  furniture makers, 12
  musical instrument makers, 63
  potters, 63
  stonemasons, 63
  upholsters, 1, 83
  See also Trade unions
Cyprus
  licensed individuals in, 66*t*, 67

upper and lower bound ISCO worker codes for, 64*t*, 65, 77*nn*5–6
Czech Republic, 2012 data on numbers of licenses in, 64*t*, 65, 66*t*, 76*n*4

Day, Ryan, deregulation and, 51
Decision making, 37, 72–73
Denmark
  licensed individuals in, 66*t*, 67
  upper and lower bound ISCO worker codes for, 64*t*, 65, 77*nn*5–6
Dent, Frank, credentials of, 13
Dent v. West Virginia, 13, 26
Dentists
  contested tasks of, 58, 80
  as licensed occupation, 1, 2–3, 4, 14, 48, 91
  mobility of, 31, 33, 85
  prices and, 26, 31, 37–38, 55, 81
  service quality of, 26, 38–39, 41, 81
Deregulation, 18
  construction occupations and, 22, 52
  effect on employment, 68, 81, 82
  effect on quality, 6, 52, 59*n*1, 68
  reducing growth in occupational licensing by, 5–6, 86–88
Disadvantaged populations, 3, 93
  See also Low-income populations
District of Columbia (DC)
  licensed occupations in, 22, 25
  nonlicensed occupations in, and parts fraud, 40–41
Doctors. *See* Physicians
Dues collection by professional associations, 14

Earnings, 20, 25, 57
  licensed *vs.* unlicensed occupations and, 7*n*1, 30–31, 55
  restricted supply of practitioner and, 16, 57–58
Economic theory, monopolies in, 11, 36–37, 79, 83
Education, 39, 65
  credentials from, and training (*see under* Licensing requirements, specific education and testing)

Index 109

Education occupations, teachers, 2–3, 31, 39, 43–44, 63
See also various instructors under Sports occupations
Employers, 11–12, 62, 75
Employment, 47
certificates and, decision making, 72–73
effect of deregulation on, 6, 68, 82
licensing effect on, 7, 25, 26, 31, 43, 80
unions and, benefits, 11–12
Estonia
2012 data on numbers of licenses in, 64t, 65, 66t, 76n4
licensed individuals in, 66t, 67
European Union (EU), occupational licensing in, 2, 7, 61–68
focus and requirements of, 62–63
licensed individuals in each EU-27 country, 65–67, 66t, 76nn2–4, 77nn5–6
licensed professions in each EU-27 country, 63–65, 64t, 76n1
perceived overregulation in, 67, 88–89
See also specific countries, e.g., Poland
Eurostat, coding schemes of, 65, 76n3, 77n5
Expanding Opportunity in America (Ryan), 85

Featherbedding, dental industry and, 91
Federal Trade Commission, North Carolina State Board of Dental Examiners v., 37–38
Federal Trade Commission (FTC), 6
overuse of licensed services found by, 40–41, 43
Federation of State Medical Boards, AMA and, 16
Financial industry
accountants in, 72, 75, 77n8
brokers in, 63–64
credit card providers, 88
Finland, licensed individuals in, 66t, 67

Flexner Report (Flexner), AMA sponsorship of, 15, 16, 17
Florida, 29f, 57, 94n3
France, licensed individuals in, 66t, 67
Fraud, 90
service quality vs., 41, 93
Free to Choose (Friedman and Friedman), 10–11, 23n1, 98
Friedman, Milton
on cost of quality, 5, 16–17
on political economy, 10–11, 23n1, 79, 98
Friedman, Rose, on political economy, 10–11, 23n1, 98
FTC. See Federal Trade Commission
Funeral occupations
florists, 1
funeral directors, 14

Georgia, 29f, 51–52, 94n3
Germany
licensed individuals in, 66t, 67
upper and lower bound ISCO worker codes for, 64t, 65, 77nn5–6
Government regulation, 1
incentives for, 4–7
as market intervention, 25–26
monopolies and, 11, 36–37, 79, 82–83
reciprocity of, 2–3, 32, 80, 82, 94n3
See also U.S. law and legislation
Grandfather clauses, time of hire important in, 30, 70
Greece
licensed individuals in, 66t, 67
upper and lower bound ISCO worker codes for, 64t, 65, 77nn5–6
Grievance procedures, as voice effect benefit, 11
Guilds, medieval times and, 4, 12, 22

Harris Poll Interactive, survey projects of, 27–28, 28t
Hawaii, workforce licensed in, 29f, 57
Health care, 90, 91
ancient Greece and, 10, 22
insurance reimbursements for, 48, 54, 85–86

110 Kleiner

Health care, *cont.*
  medical services and prices in, 40, 81
  overlapping occupations within, and task allocation, 47–50, 53–54, 56, 58
Health care occupations
  anesthesiology assistants, 5
  behavioral and medical counselors, 5, 74
  dietitians and nutritionists, 5, 74
  eye care, 41, 85
  nurses, 14, 31, 47–48, 63, 75
  occupational therapists (OTs), 47, 53–58, 85–86
  paramedics, 1, 11, 28
  pharmacists, 75
  physical therapists (PTs), 1, 23–24n3, 47, 53–58, 88
  podiatrists, 63
  respiratory therapists, 4
  surgeons, 10, 92–93
  See also Dentists; Physicians
Health care occupations, substitutes in
  dental hygienists, 17, 28, 35, 41, 55, 58, 80, 81, 91
  nurse practitioners, 17, 35, 47, 48–50, 55, 58, 80
  nurse's aides, 3
  physician's assistants, 47, 55
Hippocratic Oath, 10–11, 22
Hospitality occupations
  bartenders, 61
  tour guides, 1, 3, 6
  travel agents, 3, 63
Human resources occupations
  employment agents, 6, 73
  managers, 74

Idaho, licensing legislation vetoed in, 5, 25
Illinois, 4, 29f, 49
Income inequality, 37, 85
Indiana
  licensed workforce in, 29, 29f
  licensure legislation in, 5, 15, 25, 87–88
Industrial occupations
  boilermakers, 41
  scrap metal recyclers, 25
  See also Manufacturing sector
Industrial Revolution, effect on enterprises and guilds, 12, 22–23
Information access, 27, 31, 33, 93
Innovation
  benefits from nonregulated services as, 90–91
  licensing effects on, 7, 17, 38, 42, 80
Institute for Justice
  licensure law and, 3, 6, 86
  survey projects of, 27–28, 28t
Insurance industry
  health care reimbursements by, 48, 56
  monetizing risk through, 42, 44
  social insurance in, 36–38, 44
Interior designers
  licensing sought by, in all states, 2, 6, 9, 21, 23, 52–53
  nonlicensed, as certified and registered, 21–22, 50–51, 53, 83
  overlapping tasks of, 20, 23, 47, 51, 58, 59n1
International licensing, 34, 36
  issues in, and policy implications, 88–89
  perspectives on, 2, 5–6, 7 (*see also* China, occupational licensing in; European Union, occupational licensing in; United Kingdom, occupational licensing in)
International product markets, local *vs.*, 12
International Standard Classification of Occupations (ISCO), 66t, 77n5
Iowa
  licensing in, 28, 29, 29f
  licensure legislation vetoed in, 5, 25
Ireland, licensed individuals in, 66t, 67
ISCO. *See* International Standard Classification of Occupations
Italy
  licensed individuals in, 66t, 67
  upper and lower bound ISCO worker codes for, 64t, 65, 77nn5–6

Jacksonian populism, few state regulations during, 13

Job creation, licensing effect on, 80
Job openings, barriers to, 30, 34–35, 44
Job skills
   appropriate, 3, 4, 93
   manual or mechanical (*see*
      Construction occupations)
Judicial and legal occupations
   attorneys, 1, 5, 6, 26, 31, 33–34, 37,
      43, 63, 75
   court clerks, 6
   notaries, 6

Kansas, workforce licensed in, 29*f*, 57

Labor markets
   advantage of certificates in, 72–73
   improving, with policy reform, 6, 61,
      79
   licensing as institution of, 2, 6–7, 9,
      25, 44, 74, 88
   outcomes in, and effect of
      occupational regulations, 54–55,
      59*n*1
   standardized inputs to, with
      technological advances, 40, 80
   supply in, 11, 30–31
Labor reform
   barriers to occupational access and,
      84–85
   certificates favored in, 86–87, 94*n*4
   cost-benefit analysis in, 81–82, 83,
      94*n*2
   federal role in, 80, 83–86
   improving markets with, 6, 61, 79
   legal principles in, during
      Progressive Era, 13–14
   potential for, 79–83
   state legislation for, 81–82, 86–87,
      94*n*2, 94*n*4
Latvia
   2012 data on numbers of licenses in,
      64*t*, 65, 66*t*, 76*n*4
   licensed individuals in, 66*t*, 67
   upper and lower bound ISCO worker
      codes for, 64*t*, 65, 77*nn*5–6
Lawyers. *See under* Judicial and legal
   occupations, attorneys

Licensed occupations, battles among,
   47–59
   construction personnel in, 47, 50–53,
      58
   health care personnel in, 47–50,
      53–58
Licenses, 3
   as government standards, 1, 69, 73
   growth of occupations that require,
      1–2
   interaction of unions with jobs that
      require, 9, 10–11, 23*n*1
   standard method for obtaining, 14–15
Licensing boards, 21, 88
   members serving on, and work
      capture, 37–38
   state, and functions, 1, 4, 16, 17, 58,
      70, 80, 87
Licensing requirements
   bonding, 20, 23
   professional investments, 33, 38, 89
   residency, 2–3, 74
   specific education and testing, 1, 2,
      3, 7*n*1, 16, 28*t*, 32, 43, 63, 70,
      73–74, 85, 89
Licensure laws, 6, 55, 70
   legal principles on, during
      Progressive Era, 13–14
   opposition to, 3, 27, 51–52
   organizational lobbying for, 4–5,
      14–15
   support of, 3–4, 51
Lithuania
   2012 data on numbers of licenses in,
      64*t*, 65, 66*t*, 76*n*4
   licensed individuals in, 66*t*, 67
Local institutions, 12
   broader than federal, in their reach,
      83, 85
   cost-benefit analysis as policy reform
      by, 81–82
   governmental licenses and, abroad,
      71, 74
Loss aversion, consumer risk prevention
   as, 36, 90
Louisiana, 29*f*, 59*n*1
   licensed occupations in, 1, 25, 40–41

Low-income populations
barriers to, 3, 34, 43, 85
licensed services affordability to, 4,
42, 43, 81
Lowery, Michael, deregulation and,
51–52

Malta, licensed individuals in, 66*t*, 67
Manufacturing sector, U.S. economy
and, 3, 12, 80
Massachusetts, 28, 29*f*
Medicare, 56, 57, 85–86
Mexico, occupational licensing in, 29*f*
MHRSS. *See* Ministry of Human
Resource and Social Security,
China
Michigan, 28, 29*f*
Microsoft (firm), legal certificates issued
by, 75
Migration
international, and licensing, 34, 89
interstate, and licensing, 31–32, 32*f*,
43–44
Ministry of Human Resource and Social
Security (MHRSS), China
certificates issued by, 74, 77*n*11
certification data from, 72–73, 77*n*10
certified licenses and, 72, 75, 77*n*12
Minnesota, 1, 29*f*
policy reform in, legislation, 81–82,
86–87, 94*n*2, 94*n*4
Missouri, 29*f*, 49–50
Mobility
reciprocity and, 2–3, 32, 82, 94*n*3
restrictions on, by licensed services,
2, 31–35, 80, 83–84
Monopolies, 11
downside of, 79, 82–83
long-term impact of, 36–37
Mortgage industry
brokers in, 9, 19–20, 23, 24*nn*4–5, 81
deregulation of, 18–19

National Conference of State
Legislatures, monitoring by, 48
National Labor Relations Act (NLRA),
12, 13
Taft-Hartley amendments to, 23*n*2, 91

National product markets, local *vs.*, 12
National regulations
deregulation of, 5–6, 68
government license to practice as, 69,
70, 73
local *vs.*, and licenses, 71, 74
Netherlands, licensed individuals in,
66*t*, 67
Nevada, 29*f*, 94*n*3
New Hampshire, licensed workforce in,
29, 29*f*
New Jersey, 29*f*, 94*n*3
New York, 28, 50, 94*n*3
workforce licensed in, 29*f*, 57
NLRA. *See* National Labor Relations Act
North Carolina, workforce licensed in, 29*f*
*North Carolina State Board of Dental
Examiners v. Federal Trade
Commission*, 37–38

Obama, Pres. Barack, advisors to, 3
Occupational access, 12, 14, 62, 68
licensed *vs.* unlicensed occupations
and, 7*n*1, 23, 24*n*4
licensing effect on, 3, 4, 7, 11, 17,
31–32, 40, 44, 70, 80, 89
reform of barriers to, and U.S.
executive branch, 84–85
standards set by specialized workers
for, 22, 57, 83
tax proposed for building barriers to,
82–83
Occupational classification systems, 66*t*,
74, 77*n*5, 77*n*11
Occupational licensing
anatomy of, 1–7
different contexts for, 27–29,
28*t*, 44–45*n*3, 70 (*see also under*
International licensing)
growth of, 1–2, 3, 9, 13, 36, 40,
85–86, 89
incentives for regulation, 4–7, 37–38,
82
international perspectives on (*see*
China, occupational licensing
in; European Union, occupational
licensing in; United Kingdom,
occupational licensing in)

Index 113

Occupational licensing, *cont.*
  net effects of, 2, 30–31, 43, 44, 57, 58, 90
  policy implications in (*see* Public policy, implications for occupational licensing)
  political economy of, 3, 10–11
  as social insurance, 36–38, 44, 85–86
  state regulation in, 1–4, 14, 54–55
  as stealth regulation, 2, 44
Occupational licensing, evolution of, 2, 9–24, 75
  case studies in, 15–22, 23
  deregulation and reducing growth in, 5–6
  history of, in fact and literature, 9–15, 22–23, 41, 43, 54–55
  United States and, 12–15
Oregon, 27, 29*f*, 94*n*3
OTs. *See under* Health care occupations, occupational therapists
Otter, Gov. Butch, vetoes of, 5

Penalties
  among enforcement mechanisms, 87, 93
  working without regulatory requirement and, 69, 72, 73–74, 75
Pence, Gov. Mike, licensure legislation and, 5, 15
Pennsylvania, 94*n*3
  workforce licensed in, 29*f*, 57
People's Republic of China, occupational licensing in. *See* China, occupational licensing in
Personal care occupations
  barbers, 3, 14
  chiropractors, 17
  cosmetologists, 3, 28, 31, 43
  hair braiders, 1, 3, 83
  manicurists, 1, 3, 34, 63
  shampoo specialists, 1–2, 83
  shoe fitters, 25
  sign-language interpreters, 5
  tooth whiteners, 37–38
Physicians
  as licensed occupation, 1, 2–3, 10–11, 14, 26, 31, 47–48, 63, 73, 75
  licensing sought by, 9, 13, 15–17
  overuse of services by, 16–17
  postgraduation requirements for, 16, 17
  service quality of, 36, 40
  specialties of, 92–93
  tasks allocated to, 47, 49, 50, 58, 80
Poland
  2012 data on numbers of licenses in, 64*t*, 65, 66*t*, 76*n*4
  national labor markets to be deregulated in, 6, 68
Political economy, 13
  Milton and Rose Friedman on, 10–11, 23*n*1, 98
Politics, 13, 58
  libertarian issues in, 46, 86
  trade, in contemporary and medieval times, 4–5, 12, 14, 15, 22
Portugal, upper and lower bound ISCO worker codes for, 64*t*, 65, 77*nn*5–6
Poverty reduction, deregulation and, 85
Practice acts and bills, 21, 22, 48, 50
  See also Right to practice
Prices of goods and services, deregulation effect on, 6, 23, 68, 85
Private sector, 12, 88
Productivity, European, 61
Professional associations
  European occupations in, 65, 71
  European regulated professions database, 63, 64*t*, 76*n*4
  examination requirements of, 63, 71
  lobbying by, and licensure laws, 14–15, 23, 57
  rights to work issued by, 71, 74, 88
  unethical behavior by members of, 16–17, 37, 42, 79
  See also American Society of Interior Designers (ASID); *specifics, e.g.,* American Medical Association (AMA)
Promotions, 11, 72, 85
Protection of function, specific UK job titles and, 70–71

Protection of title, specific UK job titles and, 70, 72
PTs. See under Health care occupations, physical therapists
Public harm as occupational consequence, 3, 73
  prevention of, and licensing, 6, 12, 27, 36, 71, 80
Public health, welfare or safety, state regulation of, 13, 22, 28, 36, 83, 86–87
Public policy, 1
  assessment of nurse practitioner regulations as, 48–50
  protections in, through federal and state statutes, 12, 41, 70, 79
Public policy, implications for occupational licensing, 79–94
  decision making on task allocation in, 79–80
  downsides of, 33–35
  federal role in reform, 80, 83–86
  international issues in, 88–89
  reform potentials in, 79–83
  state level in, 86–88
  United States and, 89–93
Public sector, state laws for unions in, 12

Quality of goods and services
  advertising as medium for, 41, 62
  cost and, 5, 17
  deregulation effect on, 6, 52, 59n1, 68
  licensing effect on, 2, 5, 7, 26, 30, 36, 38–42, 44, 81
  perception of assurance in, 12, 36, 37, 43, 93
  practice laws and, 50, 51–52, 59n1

Realty occupations
  appraisers, 75
  real estate agents, 63
  surveyors, 72, 85
  urban planners, 75
Registrations, 65
  as nonlicensed regulation, 21–22, 50–51, 53, 73
  UK and, 71–72

Regulation of occupations
  benefits from nonregulated services, 90–91
  governments and (see Government regulation; National regulations; State regulations)
  perceived overregulation in, 67, 68–69 (see also Deregulation)
  policy assessments of, and nurse practitioners, 48–50
  types of (see Certificates; Licenses; Registrations)
Residency requirements, occupational licensing and, 2–3, 74
Rhode Island, licensed workforce in, 29, 29f
Right to practice, 83
  license for, as precondition of work, 1, 21, 69, 73
Right to title, certificate for, as government protection, 1, 21, 70, 74, 87, 91–93
Risk, 3
  loss aversion and, 36, 90
  monetizing, through insurance, 42, 44
Romania, licensed individuals in, 66t, 67
Roosevelt, Pres. Theodore, Progressive Era under, 13–14
Royal Institute of Chartered Surveyors, protection of title and, 72
Ryan, Rep. Paul, on deregulation, 85

Safety and security occupations
  body guards, 6
  locksmiths, 3, 28, 83
Seniority recognition, as voice effect benefit, 11
Service sector, 37, 74
  repair occupations in, 40–41, 63
  U.S. economy and, 3, 13, 14, 23, 80
Services licensed and their influence, 25–45
  costs of, 2, 3–4, 5, 11, 25–26, 30–31, 35, 43–44, 44n1
  geographic mobility and, 2, 31–35, 80
  quality of, 2, 5, 38–42, 44

Services licensed and their influence, cont.
   See also Licensed occupations, battles among; under specific categories, e.g., Health care occupations; Personal care occupations
Sherman Antitrust Act, 13, 37
Slovenia, 2012 data on numbers of licenses in, 64t, 65, 66t, 76n4
Social costs, licensed occupations and, 3, 36, 85
Social insurance, occupational licensing as, 36–38, 44
Spain
   licensed individuals in, 66t, 67
   upper and lower bound ISCO worker codes for, 64t, 65, 77nn5–6
Sports occupations
   athletic trainers, 28
   ballroom dance instructors, 83
   golf instructors, 63
   professional wrestlers, 1–2
   ski instructors, 63
   soccer stars, 61
State law and legislation, 12, 48
   constitutional tests for, 14, 22, 27
   cost-benefit analysis as policy reform in, 81–82, 94n2
   police powers of, and trade-offs, 13, 17, 26, 36, 90
   politics and, 13, 15, 58
   reform, with certificates favored over licenses, 86–87, 94n4
   time from, passage to labor market influence, 30–31, 43, 57, 58
State regulations
   broader than federal, in their reach, 83–84, 85
   fees for, as government revenue, 82–83
   foothold of, in Progressive Era, 14, 26
   nontransferable across state lines, 2, 13
   variation among, 74, 80, 84
Surety bonds, mortgage brokers and, 19–20, 24nn4–5

Survey data collection
   China and, 72–73, 77n9
   European Labour Force Survey, 65–67, 66t, 69, 76n4, 77n6
   European regulated professions database, 63, 64t, 76n4
Sweden
   2012 data on numbers of licenses in, 64t, 65, 66t, 76n4
   licensed individuals in, 66t, 67

Taft-Hartley amendments, NLRA among, 23n2, 91
Taxes, workers building barriers to occupational access and, 82–83
Technological advances, standardized labor inputs with, 40, 80
Templeton Foundation, survey funding by, 27
Texas, 29f, 94n3
Textile occupations, corset makers, 63
Title acts
   See also Right to title
Title acts, practice acts vs., 21
Trade unions, 47, 70
   closed shop and, 69, 91
   function of, analogous to product monopolies, 11–12
   interaction of licensing with, and impact, 2, 9, 10–11, 23n1
   NLRA and, 12, 13
Traditional trades. See Construction occupations
Transportation occupations, taxi drivers, 6, 26–27, 71

Uber (firm), licensure laws and, 26–27
UK. See United Kingdom, occupational licensing in
Unemployment, 61, 80
Unethical behaviors
   fraud as, 41, 90, 93
   income and, 16–17, 37, 42, 79
United Kingdom (UK), occupational licensing in, 12, 68–72
   documentation in, 67, 68–69
   growth of, 69–70
   institutional details of, 70–72

United Kingdom (UK), occupational
  licensing in, *cont.*
    licensed individuals in, 65–67, 66*t*,
      76*nn*2–4, 77*nn*5–6
    licensed professions in, 64*t*, 68–69,
      76*n*1, 77*n*7
    wage effects of, 69, 89, 91
United States
  manufacturing and service economies
    in, 3, 12–13, 14
  occupational licensing perspective
    in, 2, 5–6, 7, 13–14, 29*f*, 41–42,
    62, 89 (*see also specific states,
    e.g.,* Louisiana; Minnesota)
  U.S. Dept. of Defense, reform and,
    84–85
  U.S. Dept. of the Treasury, reform and,
    84
  U.S. law and legislation, 86
    licensed occupations in, 13, 37–38
    unions in, 12, 23*n*2
  U.S. Supreme Court, state right to grant
    upheld by, 13

Veterinary occupations
  horse tooth filers, 1
  horseshoers, 14
  pet groomers, 83
Voice effect, labor market supply and, 11

Wages, 11, 22, 33
  growth of, 3–4, 7*n*1
  job skills and, 3, 4
  licensing impact on, 2, 3, 7, 9, 11, 36,
    43, 59*n*2, 69–70, 73, 75
  time needed for law to influence,
    30–31, 43, 57, 58, 69–70, 89
  trade unions and, 12, 70, 91
Washington, D.C. *See* District of
  Columbia
Washington (State)
  commendable reciprocity between,
    and California, 94*n*3
  high share of workforce licensed in,
    29*f*
West Virginia, Dent v., 13, 26
West Virginia, workforce licensed in, 29*f*

Workforce
  certificates as, advantage in labor
    markets, 72–73
  EU-27, with license requirement,
    63–67, 64*t*, 66*t*, 90
  job advancement for (*see* Promotion)
  licensing benefits to, 3–4
  mobility of, 2, 31–35, 43, 80, 85
  as nonunion *vs.* union employees,
    11–12
  as supply in labor market, 11,
    25–26, 30–31, 55, 81, 91 (*see
    also* Occupational access)
  U.S., with license requirement,
    27–29, 28*t*, 29*f*, 67, 90

About the Institute

The W.E. Upjohn Institute for Employment Research is a nonprofit research organization devoted to finding and promoting solutions to employment-related problems at the national, state, and local levels. It is an activity of the W.E. Upjohn Unemployment Trustee Corporation, which was established in 1932 to administer a fund set aside by Dr. W.E. Upjohn, founder of The Upjohn Company, to seek ways to counteract the loss of employment income during economic downturns.

The Institute is funded largely by income from the W.E. Upjohn Unemployment Trust, supplemented by outside grants, contracts, and sales of publications. Activities of the Institute comprise the following elements: 1) a research program conducted by a resident staff of professional social scientists; 2) a competitive grant program, which expands and complements the internal research program by providing financial support to researchers outside the Institute; 3) a publications program, which provides the major vehicle for disseminating the research of staff and grantees, as well as other selected works in the field; and 4) an Employment Management Services division, which manages most of the publicly funded employment and training programs in the local area.

The broad objectives of the Institute's research, grant, and publication programs are to 1) promote scholarship and experimentation on issues of public and private employment and unemployment policy, and 2) make knowledge and scholarship relevant and useful to policymakers in their pursuit of solutions to employment and unemployment problems.

Current areas of concentration for these programs include causes, consequences, and measures to alleviate unemployment; social insurance and income maintenance programs; compensation; workforce quality; work arrangements; family labor issues; labor-management relations; and regional economic development and local labor markets.

CPSIA information can be obtained
at www.ICGtesting.com
Printed in the USA
FSOW03n1410090916
24799FS